THE ULTIMATE SPURS QUIZ BOOK

1,250 Questions Covering the 80s, 90s and 2000s

Compiled by Chris Cowlin
Foreword by Chas Hodges

UNOFFICIAL AND UNAUTHORISED

APEX PUBLISHING LTD

This book was first published in hardback in 2010 and was updated in 2014, 2015 and 2016 and re-published in paperback by:

Apex Publishing Ltd
12A St. John's Road, Clacton on Sea, Essex, CO15 4BP, England
www.apexpublishing.co.uk

British Library Cataloguing-in-Publication Data
A catalogue record for this book is available from the British Library

ISBN: 978-1-78538-476-9

Typeset in 10.5pt Arial
Cover design and image: Chris Cowlin

Special Note: *This book is in no way connected to Tottenham Hotspur Football Club. It is unofficial and unauthorised.*

Dedication:
*This book is dedicated to my dad, Martin. We have been to many Spurs matches together - some great memories.
Also, to Harry, Aimee and Hannah - all big Spurs fans!*

CONTENTS

FOREWORD

I never became a Spurs fan; I was born a Spurs fan - just around the corner from the ground, in the North Middlesex Hospital, Edmonton, in 1943. If I'd been born a bit further down the road, I would've been born an Arsenal fan! That's the way it was in those days. You supported your local team. I still do a double take when someone younger than me states in a cockney accent that he supports "Man U". It doesn't make sense.

I first went 'up the Spurs' with my older brother, Dave, around 1954, but not to see the first team. Back in those days there was a reserve match every other week, which would pull around five to six thousand people, compared with the forty to fifty thousand at first team matches. Mum was worried about our safety among the huge crowds, so she would only let us go to reserve matches. Then we turned up one Saturday to find that the first team were playing. When we got home we told mum what a great time we'd had and how we were now "old enough to look after ourselves among big crowds". So from then on we were allowed to go up the Spurs with the big boys.

I played in goal for Eldon Road School and the Spurs goalie then, Ted Ditchburn, was my hero. He'd played a couple of games for England, but I thought he should've been England's permanent goalkeeper. Alf Ramsey was Spurs' left back at that time. Whenever he got the ball he always did something useful with it. A master penalty taker, I never saw him miss. I remember Danny Blanchflower's first game. He didn't kick a ball, he placed it, like a chess player. Some of Glenn Hoddle's style later on reminded me of Danny.

When music took over and I began to learn guitar in 1956, Spurs took a back seat. Although I've always had a warm feeling for Spurs and am pleased when they're doing well, music has always come first. I never ever saw the Double side in the sixties live, as I was on the road touring and enjoying the life. I still am. I remember my mum one day saying, "You coming down the road to see the Spurs parade the Double?" But I was too busy learning a new Jerry Lee bit on the piano. Nevertheless, Spurs are in my blood and always will be.

Leaping on to the eighties, Dave and me were signed to a management company run by Bob England, a massive Spurs fan. Every time you spoke to him on the phone, the first five - or sometimes thirty - minutes were given over to opinions and critical rundowns of Tottenham's last match. Then business would start. I remember touring Australia in the eighties in the days of not-so-good electrical means of communication and Bob ringing up a pal and asking him to put the phone next to his radio for the whole second half of a Spurs commentary. I don't know what the bill was. Come to think of it, he phoned from my hotel room. I've … no, too late now.

It was Bob who suggested we should write a song for Spurs. 'Ossie's Dream' was his suggestion for a title. "That's the buzz going on down the Spurs," said Bob. "Ossie's dream is to play at Wembley."

Dave and me agreed to the idea in principle, but I had other things on my mind. I was doing string arrangements, brass arrangements … we were in the middle of an album, for Christ's sake!

So Dave took over. He came up with: "Ossie's going to Wembley/His knees have gone all Trembley." I thought the 'Trembley' bit was sort of 'dunno about that', and Dave wasn't 100% sure either - "but I can't think of anything else that rhymes with Wembley," he said. Then Bob informed us that the team played the demo on the coach and fell about. So 'Trembley' was in.

In the recording studio I spoke to Ossie.

"This is your solo bit: 'In de cup for Tottingham'," I said.

Ossie replied, "But I can say 'Tottenham' now."

"But we want you to say 'Tottingham!' The way you used to say it!"

And so he did - magnificently.

But by far the funniest line we ever got anybody to sing was Nico Clausen's line on the B side of 'Hot Shot Tottenham' (1987 Cup final). It was supposed to be funny, but Nico's unawareness made it unforgettably so. And so was Ossie's reaction, actually collapsing with laughter on the studio floor. Nico Clausen looked a little bit annoyed. He didn't really know what was going on.

Nico's line to Ossie was: "Are you gonna play a blinder?" But his delivery was so hilarious that the whole Spurs team collapsed with laughter. Ossie's response was supposed to be: "I do my best for Tottingham, mate." But Ossie couldn't get it out! We had to overdub it later.

Nico couldn't see the funny side of it, which made it even funnier. He was Belgian. 'Play a blinder?' What the (!) did that mean? But it wasn't the line, it was the way he'd done it!

Spurs lost to Coventry that year, so the record never sold a lot, which means that today that Spurs record is the most collectable because not many were pressed up. So if you've got a copy, look after it! But play the B side every now and then and fall about at dear ol' Nico's line.

So there you are. It was all fun and good football. Even the bad times were good. And, by the way, let me tell you, those boys loved it on Top of the Pops! What a team!

And now, at last, here is a quiz book that is devoted to the finest football club in the world: Tottenham Hotspur!

Best wishes
Chas Hodges

INTRODUCTION

I would first of all like to thank Chas Hodges for writing the foreword to this book; Chas and Dave have performed some great songs for Tottenham over the years so I was delighted when he agreed to write a piece for the book.

I would also like to thank all the former players, newspapers, magazines, etc, for their kind comments about this book.

Tottenham Hotspur Football Club has been a big part of my life, supporting them since I was 10 years old when I was first introduced to Spurs from my school friend Tom Luesley. It was a good choice as most of my family supported Arsenal, and still do!

My first match to 'The Lane' was in May 1994, a 2-1 defeat against QPR, the final day of the 1993/1994 season.

The 1994/1995 season remains my favourite season as a Spurs fan, seeing Jürgen Klinsmann play was tremendous and very memorable. I will never forget the game against Aston Villa in November 1994, a 4-3 defeat, Gerry Francis' first game in charge at the club – what a game that was; my Dad and I have never been off our seats so much!

I have met a lot of Spurs players over the years and Jürgen Klinsmann still remains my favourite, he always had time for the fans and is a true gentleman.

This book is focused on the last 30 years of football – covering the 1980s, 1990s and 2000s; I would like to think it has something in it for everyone.

This book has been a real joy to compile and I hope you enjoy testing your knowledge of this great club. Hopefully it should bring back some wonderful memories!

In closing, I would like to thank all my friends and family for encouraging me to complete this book.

Best wishes
Chris Cowlin

THE AUTHOR - CHRIS COWLIN

Chris Cowlin is an author, actor and entrepreneur. Born in London in 1980, Chris has achieved a great deal in a short space of time. With a background in printing and advertising, Chris owns a successful publishing company and is himself the author of 126 books. Chris has written on a range of subjects but specialises in football, sport, television and music. His books have been endorsed by many celebrities and sports personalities such as Jonathan Ross, Sir Alex Ferguson, Gary Mabbutt and Gary Lineker. His writing credits include a foreword for a book by notorious criminal, Charles Bronson, who Chris visited in prison on two occasions. He is also a regular contributor to The Sun, Daily Mirror and the letters page of local newspapers.

A keen runner, Chris took part in the London marathon in 2012 and was shortlisted to carry the Olympic Flame in the same year. He regularly competes in running events across the UK and has raised over £35,000 for various charities.

Chris also works as an actor, model and voice over artist. He has been involved in over 200 productions in the last two years including his personal highlight, appearing as an extra in the 2012 James Bond film, Skyfall.

During his career, Chris has appeared in hundreds of newspaper and magazine articles and been interviewed on radio stations across the UK, promoting his books and charity work. He actively participates in social media and has over half a million followers on Twitter.

Chris has been involved in many local community events in recent years; a former local councillor, elected in March 2012, having a majority of 798 votes, beating both the Conservative Party and the Labour Party. He was also a very active school governor between 2010 and 2012.

Chris has two children, Harry and Aimee. He is a Tottenham Hotspur season ticket holder and has written various books on his favourite team.

Visit Chris's website: www.chriscowlin.co.uk or contact him: cowlinchristopher@gmail.com or follow him on Twitter: @ChrisCowlin

QUESTIONS:

JÜRGEN KLINSMANN
1. Which Spurs manager signed Jürgen when he joined the club in 1994?
2. How many League goals did Jürgen score for Tottenham during the 1994/95 season, having played in 41 matches?
3. Against which team did Jürgen score his first goal for Spurs, in a 4-3 away win on his debut in the Premier League?
4. Against which team did Jürgen score a brace for Tottenham, in a 2-1 win on his home debut?
5. Jürgen signed on loan from which club when he joined Spurs for his second playing spell in December 1997?
6. Who was Jürgen's strike partner at Spurs during the 1994/95 season?
7. In which year was Jürgen born – 1962, 1963 or 1964?
8. How many League goals has Jürgen scored for Spurs in his career – 29, 39 or 49?
9. Which German team did Jürgen join when he left White Hart Lane in May 2005 after his first spell at the club?
10. In what year did Jürgen become manager of Germany?

HARRY REDKNAPP
11. True or false: Harry once played a League game for Spurs during his playing days?
12. In what year did Harry take charge at White Hart Lane?
13. Harry took over from which manager at White Hart Lane?
14. Harry led Spurs to the final of which Cup in his first season at the club?
15. Which team did Spurs beat 2-0 at home when Harry managed the club for the first time in the Premier League?
16. Which Tottenham chairman appointed Harry as club manager?
17. Which striker did Harry sign for Spurs from his previous club, Portsmouth, during July 2009?
18. Can you name the London club that Harry has both played for and managed in his career?

19. In which year was Harry born in London – 1945, 1946 or 1947?
20. To what position in the Premier League did Harry guide Tottenham during his first season in charge at the club?

2009/2010

21. Which team did Spurs beat 2-1 on the opening day of the League season at White Hart Lane?
22. Which striker scored a Spurs hat-trick in a 5-1 away League win against Hull City during August 2009?
23. Which team did Tottenham beat 5-0 at home, with Robbie Keane grabbing four of the goals, during September 2009?
24. How many of Tottenham's nine goals did Jermain Defoe score in their 9-1 home League win against Wigan Athletic during November 2009?
25. With which London team did Spurs share a 0-0 away draw on Boxing Day 2009?
26. Can you name Tottenham's two goalscorers in the 2-0 home League win over West Ham during December 2009?
27. Which striker came off the bench to score a brace away at Wigan Athletic in Tottenham's 3-0 League win?
28. Which French defender did Spurs sign from Newcastle United during August 2009?
29. For which club did Darren Bent sign when he left White Hart Lane in August 2009?
30. Who wore the number 15 shirt for Tottenham during this season?

HONOURS

Match up the honour with the year it was achieved

31.	FA Cup Winners	2008
32.	Charity Shield Winners (joint)	2005
33.	League Cup Winners	1984
34.	Charity Shield Winners (joint)	1990
35.	FA Cup Winners	1992
36.	Peace Cup (Korea) Winners	1991
37.	League Cup Winners	1982
38.	FA Youth Cup Winners	1981
39.	FA Cup Winners	1999

LEGENDS – 1
Rearrange the letters to reveal the name of a club legend
41. LENNG OLDHED
42. DEDYT HIGHERMANS
43. SISOE DERAILS
44. KYRCI LAVLI
45. VADDI INGOAL
46. YGRA BABTTUM
47. NEARJIM FEEDO
48. ARY CELMENEC
49. RHGTA ORSOCK
50. AIN ELKWAR

FA CUP WINNERS – 1991
51. Which team did Spurs beat in the FA Cup final?
52. Who played in goal for Tottenham in the FA Cup final?
53. What was the score in the FA Cup final?
54. Which England left back put the opponents 1-0 up, scoring a trademark free kick?
55. Can you name the two substitutes that Spurs used in the FA Cup final?
56. Which goalkeeper saved Gary Lineker's penalty in the FA Cup final?
57. Can you name seven of Tottenham's starting eleven in the FA Cup final?
58. Which opponents' defender scored an own goal in extra time, giving Tottenham their second and winning goal in the FA Cup final?
59. Which Tottenham manager guided the club to this success?
60. Which London rivals did Spurs beat in the FA Cup semi-final at Wembley?

MANAGERS
Match up the manager with the year he took charge at White Hart Lane
61. Terry Venables   1993
62. Gerry Francis   1992
63. George Graham   2004

64.	Glenn Hoddle	1987
65.	Martin Jol	1986
66.	Christian Gross	1994
67.	Doug Livermore	1997
68.	Juande Ramos	1998
69.	David Pleat	2001
70.	Ossie Ardiles	2007

FIRST PREMIER LEAGUE SEASON – 1992/1993

71. With which club did Spurs share a 0-0 away draw in their first ever Premier League match during August 1992?
72. True or false: Spurs had to wait until their sixth Premier League match before they recorded their first win?
73. Which striker scored a brace against Arsenal at Highbury in a 3-1 win during May 1993?
74. How many of their 42 Premier League matches did the club win – 12, 14 or 16?
75. Which striker did Spurs sign from Nottingham Forest during August 1992?
76. Against which team did Teddy Sheringham score a Spurs hat-trick in a 4-0 home League win during February 1993?
77. Which team did Spurs beat 4-2 at home during February 1993, scoring all their goals in five minutes, having been 1-0 down after an Iain Dowie goal?
78. Who scored Tottenham's goal in a 1-1 draw against Manchester United at White Hart Lane in the Premier League during September 1992?
79. In what position in the Premier League did Spurs finish?
80. Which striker scored a brace for Spurs in a 5-1 home win against Norwich City in the Premier League during April 1993?

LEAGUE GOALS – 1

Match up the player with the number of League goals he scored in his Tottenham career

81.	Chris Armstrong	18
82.	Darren Anderton	60
83.	Paul Allen	10
84.	Nico Claesen	20
85.	Sol Campbell	34
86.	Guy Butters	27

87.	Darren Bent	48
88.	Dimitar Berbatov	18
89.	Nick Barmby	1
90.	Clive Allen	23

WHERE DID THEY COME FROM? – 1

Match up the player with his previous club before joining Tottenham

91.	Niko Kranjčar	Southampton
92.	Carlo Cudicini	Charlton Athletic
93.	David Bentley	PSV Eindhoven
94.	Aaron Lennon	Cardiff City
95.	Danny Murphy	Portsmouth
96.	Edgar Davids	Leeds United
97.	Gareth Bale	Chelsea
98.	Darren Bent	Blackburn Rovers
99.	Chris Gunter	Inter Milan
100.	Heurelho Gomes	Charlton Athletic

JERMAIN DEFOE

101. What is Jermain's middle name – Colin, Chesney or Conroy?
102. From which London club did Jermain sign when he joined Spurs in 2004?
103. What squad number did Jermain wear for Tottenham during the 2009/10 season?
104. Which team did Spurs beat 4-3 at home, with Jermain scoring the club's first goal on his League debut during February 2004?
105. For which team did Jermain sign when he left White Hart Lane in January 2008 before returning to The Lane in January 2009?
106. For which London team did Jermain play between 1999 and 2004?
107. Against which team did Jermain score a winning 45th-minute goal for Tottenham before getting sent off after 60 minutes in a 2-1 away League win during October 2009?
108. Against which team did Jermain score a hat-trick in Tottenham's 3-1 away win in the FA Cup 4th round replay during February 2010?

109. How many League goals did Jermain score for Spurs during the 2004/05 season – 9, 11 or 13?
110. Against which country did Jermain score a brace in England's 2-2 friendly away match during August 2009?

TEDDY SHERINGHAM
111. Against which team did Teddy score his first Spurs League goal, in a 2-0 home win in the Premier League during August 1992?
112. How many League hat-tricks did Teddy score for Spurs in his first season at White Hart Lane?
113. For which club did Teddy play in between his two playing spells at Tottenham?
114. Can you name the other two London clubs that Teddy played for in his football career?
115. How many League goals did Teddy score for Spurs in his 42 appearances during the 1994/95 season – 16, 18 or 20?
116. In which year was Teddy born in London – 1965, 1966 or 1967?
117. Against which team did Teddy score a League hat-trick in Tottenham's 4-0 home win during December 1994, with Gica Popescu scoring Spurs' other goal in the game?
118. How many League appearances did Teddy make for Spurs in his playing days – 236, 239 or 242?
119. Which Spurs manager signed Teddy in 2001 for his second playing spell at The Lane, this being one of the manager's first signings?
120. How many League goals did Teddy score in his Tottenham career – 95, 97 or 99?

2008/2009
121. Which Spurs midfielder scored a brace in a 4-0 home win against Middlesbrough during March 2009?
122. What was the score when Spurs visited The Emirates Stadium to play Arsenal during October 2008?
123. Which striker scored a brace when Spurs beat Wigan 3-1 during January 2009 at White Hart Lane?
124. Who started the League season as Tottenham manager but was replaced in October 2008?

125. Which French defender joined Tottenham for his second spell at the club during January 2009, signing from Sunderland?
126. Which striker finished the season as the club's highest scorer with 12 League goals?
127. Which team did Spurs beat 2-1, with Roman Pavlyuchenko scoring a 90th-minute winner, during November 2008?
128. Which goalkeeper did Spurs sign on a free transfer from Chelsea during January 2009?
129. Which Spurs player scored the only goal in a 1-0 home win over West Ham United at White Hart Lane during April 2009?
130. In what position in the Premier League did Spurs finish – 7th 8th or 9th

OSSIE ARDILES
131. How many League goals did Ossie score for Tottenham in his career – 6, 16 or 26?
132. Ossie appeared in which 1981 film alongside football legends Pelé and Bobby Moore?
133. Against which team did Ossie make his Spurs debut, in a 1-1 League away draw during August 1978?
134. Can you name the three English sides that Ossie played for after leaving Tottenham, in the late 1980s?
135. True or false: Ossie wore the number 1 shirt for his country in the 1982 World Cup?
136. How many League goals did Ossie score for Spurs during the 1980/81 season?
137. Can you name the three winners' medals that Ossie won whilst a Tottenham player?
138. How many League games did Ossie play for Tottenham in his playing career – 238, 258 or 278?
139. In what year was Ossie appointed as Tottenham manager?
140. What nationality is Ossie?

LES FERDINAND
141. How many England caps did Les win for England, scoring five goals?

142. Against which London team did Les score the 10,000th goal in Premier League history during December 2001 in a 4-0 home win for Spurs?
143. Against which team did Les score a Spurs hat-trick in a 6-0 home win in the League Cup quarter-final during December 2001?
144. Which Spurs manager signed Les for Tottenham in 1997?
145. Against which London team did Les score his first Tottenham League goal, in only his second game for the club, in a 2-1 away defeat during August 1997?
146. In what position did Les play during his playing days?
147. How many League goals did Les score for Spurs in his career – 22, 33 or 44?
148. Against which Midlands club did Les score a brace for Spurs in a 3-2 home League win during August 1997?
149. What was the only medal that Les won whilst a player at White Hart Lane?
150. From which team did Les join Tottenham in 1997?

2007/2008
151. In what position did Spurs finish in the League this season?
152. Can you name the two strikers that finished the season with 15 League goals?
153. With which London team did Tottenham draw 4-4 at White Hart Lane in the League during March 2008?
154. Which striker scored a brace for Spurs in a 4-0 home win in the Premier League during March 2008?
155. Which Brazilian defender did Spurs sign from German side Hertha Berlin during January 2008?
156. What was the score when Manchester United visited White Hart Lane in the Premier League during February 2008?
157. Which Spurs striker scored four goals against Reading in Tottenham's 6-4 League win at The Lane during December 2007?
158. Which two players both scored a brace for Spurs in their 5-1 home win against Fulham on Boxing Day 2007?
159. Which defender did Spurs sign from Middlesbrough during January 2008?

160. Which French defender scored Tottenham's last-minute equaliser in a 4-4 home League draw during October 2007?

LEAGUE APPEARANCES – 1
Match up the player with the number of League appearances he made for Spurs in his career

161.	David Tuttle	37 (22)
162.	Terry Yorath	20 (6)
163.	Sergei Rebrov	48 (13)
164.	David Kerslake	257 (2)
165.	Kazuyuki Toda	45 (2)
166.	Luke Young	10 (3)
167.	Andy Reid	44 (4)
168.	Ian Walker	34 (3)
169.	Neil Ruddock	44 (14)
170.	Teemu Tainio	2 (2)

POT LUCK – 1
171. What are Tottenham's two nicknames?
172. In what year did Daniel Levy replace Alan Sugar as club chairman?
173. What does the club's Latin motto 'Audere est Facere' mean?
174. Which company were the shirt sponsors between 1995 and 1999, taking over from Holsten?
175. How many times did the club win the FA Cup during the 1980s?
176. Spurs won the League Cup four times, but in which years?
177. Can you name the first ever French manager to take charge of Spurs in their history?
178. Who was voted the club's Player of the Year for the 2009/10 season?
179. In which part of London are Spurs situated – central, north or south?
180. In which season did Spurs win the FA Premier Reserve League South Championship – 2003/04, 2005/06 or 2007/08?

CHRIS ARMSTRONG

181. How many League goals did Chris score for Tottenham in his career – 48, 58 or 68?
182. From which club did Spurs sign Chris during June 1995 for £4.5 million?
183. True or false: it took Chris until his 9th League match for Spurs to score his first Tottenham League goal?
184. Against which team did Chris score a brace in a 4-1 home League win on New Year's Day 1996?
185. In which year was Chris born in Newcastle – 1970, 1971 or 1972?
186. Against which team did Chris score a Tottenham brace in a 2-0 away League win during August 1996?
187. How many of Tottenham's goals did Chris score in the 7-2 home League win against Southampton during March 2000?
188. For which Welsh team did Chris play between 1989 and 1991?
189. Against which team did Chris score Spurs' only goal in the 23rd minute at The Lane in a 1-0 home League win during January 2000?
190. Which Spurs manager signed Chris for Tottenham?

LEAGUE APPEARANCES – 2

Match up the player with the number of League appearances he made for Spurs in his career

191. Dean Richards   29 (4)
192. Jamie Redknapp   16 (2)
193. Garry Brady   46 (8)
194. Gary Lineker   3 (10)
195. Erik Edman   12 (8)
196. Moussa Saïb   0 (9)
197. Kevin Scott   31
198. John Scales   37 (11)
199. Johnnie Jackson   105
200. Øyvind Leonhardsen   73

LEGENDS – 2

Re-arrange the letters to reveal the name of a club legend
201. LUPA NEALL
202. IBEBRO ENKEA

203. YELLED GINK
204. EOJ ARKNINE
205. ESVET MYNAPERR
206. YGRA REINELK
207. LAUP INCAGESGO
208. VILEC NELAL
209. SHIRC HOGHUNT
210. DIDVA SOWHELL

POT LUCK - 2

211. True or false: Spurs won the FA Youth Cup during the 1989/90 season?
212. Who was the first ever foreign manager of Tottenham?
213. What nationality was manager Christian Gross?
214. Who were the club's shirt sponsors between 2002 and 2006?
215. True or false: the first ever Tottenham kit comprised a navy blue shirt and shorts?
216. Which Spurs player won the Player of the Year award for the 2008/09 season?
217. Which year marked the club's 125th anniversary - 2006, 2007 or 2008?
218. What club record transfer fee did Tottenham pay Dynamo Kiev for Sergei Rebrov in 2000?
219. In what year was the club renamed 'Tottenham Hotspur Football and Athletic Club'?
220. Who was the club's kit manufacturer between 1978 and 1980?

CLIVE ALLEN

221. True or false: Clive was a striker during his playing days at White Hart Lane?
222. Clive signed from which club when he joined Spurs in 1984?
223. In which year was Clive born in Stepney – 1961, 1963 or 1965?
224. Who was Clive's father, a former Tottenham striker in the early 1960s?
225. How many League appearances did Clive make for Spurs in his career - 85, 95 or 105?
226. What is Clive's middle name – Darren, Daniel or David?

227. Against which team did Clive make his Spurs League debut, in a 4-1 win away during August 1984, scoring twice in the game?
228. Which manager signed Clive for Tottenham?
229. How many League goals did Clive score for Spurs in his career – 40, 60 or 80?
230. For which French club did Clive sign when he left The Lane in 1988?

WHERE DID THEY COME FROM? – 2
Match up the player with his previous club before joining Tottenham

231.	Steve Hodge	Coventry City
232.	Richard Gough	Southend United
233.	Bobby Mimms	Queens Park Rangers
234.	Paul Walsh	PSV Eindhoven
235.	Steve Sedgley	Nottingham Forest
236.	Justin Edinburgh	Aston Villa
237.	Pat Van Den Hauwe	Dundee United
238.	Teddy Sheringham	Liverpool
239.	Clive Wilson	Everton
240.	Gica Popescu	Everton

GARETH BALE
241. For which country is Gareth a full international?
242. Which squad number did Gareth wear for Spurs during the 2009/10 season?
243. From which club did Gareth sign when he joined Tottenham in 2007?
244. Against which three teams did Gareth score his three Premier League goals of the 2009/10 season?
245. Against which team did Gareth score his first Tottenham goal, in a 3-3 away League draw during September 2007?
246. In which year was Gareth born in Cardiff – 1988, 1989 or 1990?
247. How many League goals did Gareth score for Spurs in his first season at the club?
248. Can you name one of the two awards that Gareth won during 2007?
249. What is Gareth's middle name – Frank, Freddie or Francis?

250. True or false: Gareth won the 'Young Player of the Year' during the 2009/10 season at The Lane?

LEAGUE GOALS – 2
Match up the player with the number of League goals he scored in his Tottenham career

251.	Simon Davies	20
252.	Stephen Kelly	13
253.	Micky Hazard	4
254.	Tony Galvin	68
255.	Gary Doherty	13
256.	Terry Fenwick	13
257.	Mark Falco	2
258.	Ilie Dumitrescu	8
259.	Ruel Fox	4
260.	Jason Dozzell	15

2006/2007
261. In what position did Spurs finish in the Premier League?
262. Which defender did Tottenham sign from Benfica during January 2007?
263. Which striker finished as the club's highest League scorer with 12 goals?
264. Can you name the two Spurs players that scored in a 2-1 home League win over Chelsea during November 2006?
265. Which London team did Tottenham beat 5-1 at The Lane during December 2006?
266. Which striker scored a brace for Spurs in a 3-2 away win against Middlesbrough during April 2007?
267. Which Spurs midfielder scored Tottenham's last-minute equaliser in a 2-2 home draw against Arsenal during April 2007?
268. Which Canadian defender scored Tottenham's winner in a 4-3 away win against West Ham during March 2007?
269. Which team did Spurs beat 2-1 at The Lane on Boxing Day 2006, with Jermain Defoe scoring a brace in the game?
270. Who played in goal for Spurs during their 38 League games of this season?

DIMITAR BERBATOV

271. For which country was Dimitar a full international when he signed for Tottenham?
272. From which German team did Dimitar join Spurs in 2006?
273. Against which team did Dimitar score his first Spurs goal, in his home League debut in a 2-0 win during August 2006?
274. Against which London team did Dimitar score a Spurs brace in a 4-0 away FA Cup 5th round win during February 2007?
275. How many of Tottenham's six goals did Dimitar score in their 6-4 home League win against Reading during December 2007?
276. In which year was Dimitar born – 1979, 1981 or 1983?
277. True or false: Dimitar scored Spurs' two goals in their FA Cup 3rd round 2-2 home draw against Reading during January 2008?
278. How many League goals did Dimitar score for Tottenham in his career – 23, 25 or 27?
279. In what year did Dimitar leave White Hart Lane to join Manchester United?
280. How much did Spurs pay for Dimitar in 2006 – £9.9 million, £10.9 million or £11.9 million?

DAVID GINOLA

281. How many League goals did David score for Spurs in his career –13, 14 or 15?
282. Which Midlands team did David join when he left White Hart Lane in 2000?
283. Which two awards did David win in 1999 whilst a Tottenham player?
284. What was the only winners' medal that David won whilst a Spurs player?
285. In which year was David born in France – 1966, 1967 or 1968?
286. True or false: David only ever started League matches for Tottenham and was never used as a substitute during his career at White Hart Lane?
287. From which club did David join Tottenham in July 1997?

288. Against which team did David score his first Tottenham goal, in a 2-0 League Cup, 2nd round, 2nd leg away win during September 1997?
289. How many League games did David play for Spurs – 99, 100 or 101?
290. Against which Yorkshire team did David score a Spurs brace in a 3-0 home League win during December 1997, scoring in the 12th and 18th minutes?

2005/2006
291. True or false: Spurs were unbeaten in their first three League matches and didn't concede a League goal?
292. Which Lancashire team did Spurs beat 2-0 on Boxing Day 2005, with Robbie Keane scoring a penalty and Jermain Defoe scoring in the last minute of the game?
293. Who scored Tottenham's goal against Arsenal in a 1-1 League away draw during April 2006?
294. Which goalkeeper played in all 38 League matches for Spurs this season?
295. With how many League goals did Robbie Keane end the season, finishing as the club's highest scorer - 16, 17 or 18?
296. In what position did Spurs finish in the Premier League?
297. Which Tottenham player scored the only goal at The Lane in their 1-0 home win against Bolton Wanderers during April 2006?
298. Which Spurs midfielder scored the club's winner at home in a 3-2 League win against Sunderland during December 2005?
299. Who was Tottenham's manager during this season?
300. Which Tottenham striker scored the club's winner in a 3-2 away win against Charlton Athletic during October 2005 after being 2-0 down?

SPURS IN THE FA CUP
301. Spurs have won this competition eight times, but can you name the years?
302. Which team beat Spurs 1-0 in the semi-finals at Wembley during the 1992/93 season?

303. Spurs drew 1-1 at home to Newcastle United in the 3rd round during December 1999, but what was the score in the 3rd round replay at St James' Park, played 10 days later?
304. In which round of the competition did Everton knock Spurs out of the FA Cup during the 1985/86 season?
305. Which team beat Tottenham 4-1 in the FA Cup semi-final at Elland Road during April 1995?
306. Which Tottenham player scored a hat-trick against Manchester City in a 4-2 away win during March 1993 in the FA Cup quarter-finals?
307. Which London team did Spurs beat 3-2 away in the quarter-finals during March 2001, with Sergei Rebrov scoring a brace and Gary Doherty scoring the other Spurs goal?
308. Can you name the Spurs striker who scored the only goal in a 1-0 away win against Reading in the 3rd round replay during January 2008?
309. Which team knocked Spurs out of the competition in the 4th round during January 2009, beating Spurs 2-1 at home?
310. In which year did Spurs finish as runners-up in this competition?

LEAGUE GOALS – 3
Match up the player with the number of League goals he scored in his Tottenham career

311.	Dean Marney	1
312.	Steed Malbranque	1
313.	Mbulelo Mabizela	31
314.	Steve Perryman	1
315.	Noé Pamarot	13
316.	Noureddine Naybet	2
317.	Nayim	1
318.	John Moncur	6
319.	Mido	11
320.	Pedro Mendes	1

WHERE DID THEY GO? – 1

Match up the player with the club he joined after leaving White Hart Lane

321.	Kevin Boateng	Liverpool
322.	Gordon Durie	Luton Town
323.	John Polston	Portsmouth
324.	Paul Walsh	Rangers
325.	Paul Stewart	Nottingham Forest
326.	John Moncur	Norwich City
327.	Phil Gray	Norwich City
328.	Richard Gough	Swindon Town
329.	Chris Gunter	Portsmouth
330.	Ian Crook	Rangers

LEAGUE GOALS – 4

Match up the player with the number of League goals he scored in his Tottenham career

331.	Andy Reid	4
332.	Graham Roberts	3
333.	Ronny Rosenthal	7
334.	Neil Ruddock	18
335.	Paul Stewart	23
336.	Paul Stalteri	28
337.	Andy Turner	2
338.	Ramon Vega	2
339.	Ricardo Villa	1
340.	Mauricio Taricco	3

SPURS IN THE LEAGUE CUP

341. Spurs have won the competition four times, but can you recall the years?
342. What was the score when Spurs played Arsenal in the semi-final, 2nd leg, at White Hart Lane during January 2008?
343. Which striker scored a Tottenham brace in the club's 4-0 home win against Chester City in the 2nd round, 1st leg, during September 1995?
344. Which defender scored a 90th-minute winner in the club's 2-1 3rd round home win against Sunderland during October 1996?

345. Which Essex side did Tottenham beat 1-0 at White Hart Lane in the quarter-finals, after extra time, with Jermain Defoe scoring after 115 minutes, during December 2006?

346. Which team did Spurs beat 5-0 at home in the 2nd round, 1st leg, during September 1990?

347. Which Spurs midfielder scored the only goal in the club's 1-0 3rd round away win against Manchester City during October 1992?

348. Which team did Spurs beat 6-0 away from home in the 2nd round during September 2004, with Frederic Kanoute (2), Robbie Keane, Jermain Defoe, Goran Bunjevčević and Anthony Gardner scoring the goals?

349. What was the score when Spurs played Doncaster Rovers away in the 2nd round during August 2009?

350. In what year during the 1980s were Spurs runner-ups in the competition?

WHERE DID THEY COME FROM? – 3

Match up the player with his previous club before joining Tottenham

351.	John Scales	Sporting Lisbon
352.	Ramon Vega	Wimbledon
353.	José Dominguez	Ipswich Town
354.	Nicola Berti	Luton Town
355.	Mauricio Taricco	Liverpool
356.	Anthony Gardner	Wimbledon
357.	Gary Doherty	Liverpool
358.	Neil Sullivan	Inter Milan
359.	Chris Perry	Cagliari
360.	Øyvind Leonhardsen	Port Vale

LEAGUE CUP FINALISTS - 2009

361. Which team beat Spurs in the final, winning 4-1 on penalties after extra time?

362. What was the score after 120 minutes played?

363. What was the attendance in the League Cup final, played at Wembley – 78,217, 83,217 or 88,217?

364. Which Tottenham opponent won the Man of the Match award in the game?

365. Who were Tottenham's two centre backs during the final?

366. Can you name two of the three Spurs substitutes used in the game?
367. Who was Tottenham's manager on the day of the League Cup final?
368. How many of Tottenham's starting eleven in the final were English?
369. In what month of the year was the final played?
370. Which team did Spurs beat 6-4 on aggregate in the semi-finals?

WHERE DID THEY GO? – 2

Match up the player with the club he joined after leaving White Hart Lane

371. Gudni Bergsson	Queens Park Rangers
372. Gica Popescu	Ipswich Town
373. Kevin Scott	Reading
374. Dean Austin	Everton
375. Ronny Rosenthal	Norwich City
376. Clive Wilson	Bolton Wanderers
377. Jason Cundy	Watford
378. Steve Slade	Barcelona
379. Darren Caskey	Crystal Palace
380. Vinny Samways	Cambridge United

LEAGUE CUP WINNERS - 2008

381. Which London team did Tottenham beat in the League Cup final at Wembley?
382. Which manager led Spurs to this success?
383. Who played in goal for Spurs in the final?
384. What was the score after 90 minutes in the final?
385. Which Spurs striker scored Tottenham's equaliser in the 70th minute from the penalty spot?
386. Can you name the two French players that started the final for Spurs?
387. True or false: the attendance in the final was 87,660?
388. Who refereed the League Cup final, played in February 2008?
389. True or false: this was the first League Cup final to be played at the new Wembley Stadium, and the first to be played in England since the old Wembley was demolished in 2000?

390. Which Spurs defender scored the club's winner in extra time, heading in from a Jermaine Jenas free kick?

WHERE DID THEY GO? – 3
Match up the player with the club he joined after leaving White Hart Lane

391. Ramon Vega	Norwich City
392. Milenko Ačimovič	Leicester City
393. Chris Perry	Hull City
394. Gary Doherty	Chelsea
395. Steffen Iversen	Southampton
396. Stephen Clemence	Lille
397. Ben Thatcher	Wolves
398. Jamie Redknapp	Charlton Athletic
399. Neil Sullivan	Watford
400. Alton Thelwell	Birmingham City

TERRY VENABLES
401. How many League goals did Terry score for Tottenham in his playing career – 3, 5 or 7?
402. True or false: Terry was Spurs manager when Tottenham won the FA Cup in 1991?
403. To what position in the League did Terry guide Spurs in his first season in charge at White Hart Lane during 1987/88?
404. Which Spurs manager signed Terry for the club in 1966?
405. How many League appearances did Terry make for Spurs in his playing career - 115, 135 or 155?
406. From which London team did Terry sign for Tottenham in 1966?
407. What is Terry's nickname?
408. Which team did Terry manage between 1994 and 1996?
409. What was the only winners' medal that Terry picked up during his playing days at White Hart Lane?
410. In which year was Terry born in Dagenham – 1941, 1942 or 1943?

2004/2005
411. Can you name the three Spurs players, all with surnames beginning with 'K', who scored in the club's 5-1 home League win against Aston Villa during May 2005?

412. What was the score when Spurs visited Norwich City at Carrow Road on Boxing Day 2004?
413. Which midfielder scored a Tottenham brace, his only Spurs career goals, in their 5-2 home League win against Everton during January 2005?
414. Which team did Tottenham play on the opening day of the League season, drawing 1-1 at White Hart Lane on 14 August 2004?
415. Which defender did Tottenham sign during January 2005 from Nottingham Forest?
416. Can you name the two strikers who scored double figures in League competition for Tottenham during this season?
417. Which goalkeeper started the two League games that Paul Robinson missed during this season, away at Middlesbrough and at home against Blackburn Rovers, both during May 2005?
418. How many of their 38 League matches did Tottenham win - 14, 16 or 18?
419. Which midfielder did Spurs sign from West Ham United during August 2004?
420. Which striker scored a hat-trick in the club's 5-1 home League win against Southampton during December 2004?

GARTH CROOKS

421. True or false: Garth was awarded an OBE in 1999 for his services to football punditry?
422. Can you name the three winners' medals that Garth won whilst a Tottenham player?
423. What is Garth's middle name – Anthony, Alistair or Arnold?
424. In what year did Garth sign for Spurs from Stoke City?
425. How many League goals did Garth score for Spurs in his first season at White Hart Lane, his best tally for Tottenham in his career?
426. Against which team did Garth make his Spurs League debut, scoring in a 2-0 home win?
427. In what position did Garth play during his playing days?
428. How many League goals did Garth score for Tottenham in his career - 46, 48 or 50?
429. True or false: Garth became the first black chairman of the Professional Footballers' Association in 1988?

430. For which team did Garth sign when he left White Hart Lane in 1985?

LEAGUE CUP WINNERS - 1999
431. Which team did Tottenham beat 1-0 at Wembley in the League Cup final?
432. Who scored Tottenham's only goal in the last minute of the final?
433. Which Spurs manager led the club to this success?
434. How many of Tottenham's starting eleven were English?
435. Which German midfielder played for Tottenham in the final?
436. In what month of the year was the final played at Wembley?
437. What was the League Cup known as when Spurs won the Cup in 1999 - Worthington Cup, Coca-Cola Cup or Carling Cup?
438. What was the attendance at the final played at Wembley - 77,892, 78,892 or 79,892?
439. Which Swiss defender wore the number 15 shirt for Spurs in the final?
440. Which London team did Spurs beat 1-0 on aggregate in the semi-finals?

DARREN ANDERTON
441. From which team did Darren join Spurs in 1992?
442. How many League goals did Darren score for Spurs in his first season at The Lane, during the 1992/93 season?
443. What was the only trophy that Spurs won whilst Darren was a Tottenham player?
444. How many League appearances did Darren make for Spurs in his career - 299, 319 or 339?
445. Against which team did Darren score his first Tottenham goal, in the 57th minute, in a 4-2 home League win during February 1993?
446. Against which Yorkshire team did Darren score a Spurs brace in a 3-1 away League win during May 1996?
447. Darren made his Spurs League debut in a 0-0 away draw during August 1992, in Tottenham's first ever Premier League match, against which team?

448. True or false: Darren scored 22 League goals for Spurs in his football career?
449. What is Darren's middle name – Robert, Roger or Ryan?
450. How many goals did Darren score for England in his 30 full international caps?

MARK FALCO
451. How many League appearances did Mark make for Spurs in his career - 174, 184 or 194?
452. Which Spurs manager handed Mark his Tottenham League debut, at the age of 18?
453. How many League goals did Mark score for Spurs in his 42 appearances during the 1984/85 season – 20, 22 or 24?
454. True or false: Mark was voted as one of the top 50 greatest Spurs players of all time in 2009?
455. In what position did Mark play during his playing days?
456. In which year was Mark born in London – 1958, 1959 or 1960?
457. How many League goals did Mark score for Tottenham in his career – 68, 78 or 88?
458. Against which team did Mark make his Spurs debut, in a 3-1 win away from home during May 1979?
459. What was the only winners' medal that Mark won in his professional playing career for Spurs?
460. For which team did Mark sign when he left The Lane in 1986?

PAUL STEWART
461. With which team did Paul start his football career, turning professional in 1981?
462. True or false: Paul scored Tottenham's first goal in the 2-1 FA Cup final win in May 1991?
463. From which club did Paul sign when he arrived at White Hart Lane during June 1988?
464. How many League goals did Paul score for Spurs during his career – 26, 28 or 30?
465. Which manager signed Paul for Tottenham in June 1988?
466. Against which team did Paul make his Spurs debut, in a 2-2 home draw during October 1988?
467. What is Paul's middle name – Andrew, Adrian or Adam?

468. How many League games did Paul play for Tottenham during his playing career – 131, 331 or 531?
469. True or false: Paul won full international caps for England during his playing career at Tottenham?
470. For which team did Paul sign when he left White Hart Lane in 1992?

PETER SHREEVES
471. True or false: Peter was Spurs' youth team manager, reserve team boss and assistant manager before taking over from Keith Burkinshaw as Tottenham manager?
472. In which year was Peter born in Neath, Wales – 1938, 1939 or 1940?
473. To what position did Peter guide Tottenham in his first League season in charge at White Hart Lane?
474. Which manager took over at Spurs when Peter left in 1986?
475. In which season during the 1990s did Peter manage Spurs?
476. True or false: Peter played professional football for Spurs during his playing career?
477. Peter was Glenn Hoddle's assistant manager at which London club between 1993 and 1996?
478. True or false: Peter managed the England national team for two matches during the 1990s?
479. In which position did Peter play during his playing days – central defender, central midfielder or inside forward?
480. How many managerial spells did Peter have at Spurs?

PAUL GASCOIGNE
481. How many League goals did Paul score for Tottenham in his career – 18, 19 or 20?
482. From which club did Tottenham sign Paul in 1988?
483. In what year did Paul leave The Lane for Italian team Lazio?
484. True or false: Paul won the BBC Sports Personality of the Year award whilst at Tottenham Hotspur, in 1990?
485. How many League goals did Paul score for Spurs in his first season at the club, during the 1988/89 season?
486. What was the only winners' medal that Paul won whilst a Spurs player?

487. In 2005 Paul had a brief spell as manager of which team, a position that lasted 39 days?
488. How many League appearances did Paul make for Tottenham in his career – 82, 92 or 102?
489. What is Paul's middle name – John, Jeremy or Justin?
490. In what position did Paul play during his playing days?

2003/2004

491. Which Spurs striker scored a hat-trick against Wolves in a 5-2 home League win during December 2003?
492. With which League team did Tottenham draw 4-4 at home during February 2004?
493. Which team did Tottenham beat 2-0 away on the last day of the League season, with Robbie Keane and Jermain Defoe scoring Spurs' goals?
494. How many of their 38 League games did the club win during this season - 13, 15 or 17?
495. Who took over as caretaker manager for the remainder of the season when Glenn Hoddle left The Lane in September 2003?
496. Which midfielder scored Tottenham's winner in a 4-3 home League win against Portsmouth during February 2004?
497. How many League goals did Robbie Keane score for Tottenham during this season, finishing as the club's top scorer?
498. Which goalkeeper played in all 38 League games during this season?
499. Can you name the midfielder that signed for Spurs during January 2004 from Sheffield United?
500. Which French midfielder, on loan from Inter Milan, scored a brace in Spurs' 4-1 home League win against Birmingham during January 2004?

RICKY VILLA

501. How many League goals did Ricky score for Tottenham in his career – 18, 22 or 26?
502. In which year was Ricky born – 1950, 1951 or 1952?
503. Which two winners' medals did Ricky win whilst a Spurs player?
504. In what position did Ricky play during his playing days?

505. Which manager signed Ricky for Tottenham?
506. What nationality is Ricky?
507. In what year did Ricky win the World Cup with his country?
508. In what season did Ricky score seven League goals for Spurs, his best League tally of his White Hart Lane career?
509. Against which team did Ricky make his goalscoring Spurs debut, in a 1-1 away draw during August 1978?
510. How many League appearances did Ricky make for Tottenham in his career - 130, 133 or 136?

CHRIS WADDLE
511. How many League goals did Chris score for Tottenham in his playing career – 33, 44 or 55?
512. For which Premier League team did Chris play between 1992 and 1996?
513. In which year was Chris born in Felling, Tyne & Wear – 1958, 1959 or 1960?
514. For which French club did Chris sign when he left Spurs in 1989?
515. How many goals did Chris score for England in his 62 full international appearances?
516. What is Chris's middle name – Ralph, Roland or Rodney?
517. Against which team did Chris play on his Spurs League debut, on the opening day of the 1985/86 season, in a 4-0 home win, with Chris scoring twice in the game?
518. How many League appearances did Chris make for Tottenham in his playing career at White Hart Lane - 118, 128 or 138?
519. From which team did Chris sign for Spurs in 1985?
520. How many League goals did Chris score for Spurs during the 1988/89 season, his highest tally in a League season whilst a Spurs player?

PAUL WALSH
521. In which year was Paul born in Plumstead, London – 1961, 1962 or 1963?
522. Against which team did Paul make his Spurs debut, in a 1-1 away draw during February 1988?

523. From which club did Paul sign when he joined Spurs in 1988 for £500,000?
524. How many League goals did Paul score for Spurs in his career – 19, 29 or 39?
525. True or false: Paul was a Chelsea fan as a young boy?
526. What was the only winners' medal that Paul won during his Spurs career?
527. In what position did Paul play during his playing days?
528. True or false: Paul won full international caps for England during his playing career?
529. For which team did Paul sign when he left The Lane in 1992?
530. How many League appearances did Paul make for Spurs in his career – 118, 128 or 138?

CHRISTIAN ZIEGE
531. What nationality is Christian?
532. In what year did Spurs sign Christian from Liverpool?
533. True or false: Christian was the first ever player with a surname beginning with 'Z' to play for Spurs?
534. How many League goals did Christian score for Tottenham in his career – 3, 5 or 7?
535. Against which London team did Christian score Tottenham's League goal after 11 minutes in a 1-1 draw at White Hart Lane during December 2002?
536. For which English team did Christian play during the 1999/2000 season?
537. How many League goals did Christian score for Spurs in his first season at the club?
538. True or false: Christian scored Tottenham's goal in the 2-1 defeat against Blackburn Rovers in the League Cup final in February 2002?
539. Which Spurs manager signed Christian to bring him to The Lane?
540. How many League appearances did Christian make for Spurs in his career – 43, 45 or 47?

2002/2003
541. Which Spurs striker scored a hat-trick in a 4-3 home League win against Everton during January 2003?

542. True or false: Spurs conceded nine goals in the final two games of the League season?
543. What was the score when Leeds United visited White Hart Lane in a League match during November 2002?
544. With which team did Spurs draw 2-2 at home on Boxing Day 2002, having been 2-0 down after 49 minutes?
545. Can you name the Spurs strike partnership that scored 25 League goals between them during this season?
546. Which goalkeeper played in all 38 League games during this season – Paul Robinson, Kasey Keller or Ian Walker?
547. How many League goals did Simon Davies score for Tottenham during this season – 5, 6 or 7?
548. Which Spurs midfielder scored the winning goal in a 2-1 home win against Birmingham City during April 2003?
549. Tottenham finished 10th in the League, a higher placing than which three other London clubs?
550. Which Tottenham striker scored the winning goal in the 85th minute in a 3-2 away win against West Bromwich Albion during April 2003?

UEFA CUP WINNERS - 1984
551. Which player scored for Spurs in the 1-1 away draw in the 1st leg in the UEFA Cup final?
552. Can you name seven of Tottenham's starting eleven in the 2nd leg, with Spurs drawing 1-1 at White Hart Lane before winning 4-3 on penalties?
553. Which Spurs manager guided the club to this success?
554. Which player scored for Tottenham in the 1-1 home draw in the 2nd leg?
555. In what month of the year were both the 1st and 2nd legs of the final played?
556. What was the attendance in the final 2nd leg, played at White Hart Lane - 46,258, 48,258 or 50,258?
557. Which Yugoslavian team did Spurs beat 2-2 on away goals in the UEFA Cup semi-finals?
558. Can you name the two Spurs goalscorers when Tottenham beat Bayern Munich 2-0 at home in the 3rd round, 2nd leg?
559. Can you name two of the four players that scored Tottenham's four penalties in the final 2nd leg, winning the competition against Anderlecht in the final?

560. Who captained Spurs in the final 2nd leg, after Steve Perryman captained in the final 1st leg?

GERRY FRANCIS
561. In what year was Gerry appointed as Spurs boss, his first game in charge being a 4-3 home defeat to Aston Villa on the day that the first ever national lottery draw took place?
562. To what position in the League did Gerry guide Tottenham during the 1996/97 season?
563. Which midfielder did Gerry sign from Newcastle United during July 1997?
564. Which team did Gerry manage between 1987 and 1991?
565. Who took over as Tottenham manager at White Hart Lane when Gerry left in November 1997?
566. True or false: Gerry played for Tottenham during his playing days?
567. In which year was Gerry born in London – 1951, 1952 or 1953?
568. Which team did Gerry manage before taking charge at White Hart Lane?
569. To which round did Gerry guide Tottenham in the 1995 FA Cup?
570. To what position in the League did Gerry guide Spurs in his first season in charge at The Lane?

GLENN HODDLE
571. How many League goals did Glenn score for Spurs in his career – 66, 77 or 88?
572. In what year was Glenn appointed as Spurs manager?
573. What was the name of the single that Glenn released with another former Spurs player, Chris Waddle, in 1987?
574. How many League appearances did Glenn make for Tottenham during his career - 317, 347 or 377?
575. Which Spurs manager handed Glenn his Spurs debut, against Norwich City during August 1975?
576. For which French team did Glenn sign when he left The Lane in 1987?
577. True or false: Glenn scored 19 League goals for Spurs during the 1979/80 season?
578. How many times did Glenn win an FA Cup winners' medal whilst a Spurs player?

579. In which year was Glenn born in Hayes, Middlesex – 1956, 1957 or 1958?
580. Which team did Glenn manage between 1996 and 1999?

CHRIS HUGHTON
581. In what position did Chris play during his playing days?
582. How many full international caps did Chris win for the Republic of Ireland – 43, 53 or 63?
583. How many times did Chris win the FA Cup whilst a Spurs player?
584. How many League goals did Chris score for Spurs during the 1982/83 season?
585. For which London team did Chris sign when he left White Hart Lane in 1990?
586. For which team was Chris appointed manager in 2009?
587. How many League goals did Chris score for Spurs in his career - 12, 14 or 16?
588. Against which team did Chris make his Tottenham debut, in a 2-1 home win during September 1979?
589. In which year was Chris born in London – 1957, 1958 or 1959?
590. How many League appearances did Chris make for Spurs in his career - 293, 295 or 297?

2001/2002
591. Which defender did Tottenham purchase from Southampton for over £8 million during September 2001?
592. Can you name the two Spurs players that finished the League season with 10 goals apiece?
593. Which goalkeeper started 29 League matches during this season?
594. Which midfielder scored the club's equaliser in the 90th minute in a 1-1 home draw with Arsenal during November 2001?
595. How many of their 38 League matches did Tottenham win - 14, 15 or 16?
596. Which goalkeeper did Tottenham sign from Rayo Vallecano during August 2001?
597. Who was manager of Tottenham during this season, his first full season in charge at White Hart Lane?

598. Which midfielder scored Spurs' only goal in a 1-0 home win over Liverpool during April 2002?
599. Which team beat Spurs 5-3 at home during September 2001, Spurs having been 3-0 up at half-time?
600. How many League goals did Les Ferdinand score for Spurs during this season – 7, 8 or 9?

TOM HUDDLESTONE
601. From which team did Tom sign for Tottenham during 2005?
602. Which England manager handed Tom his full England debut in 2009?
603. How many League goals did Tom score for Spurs during the 2007/08 season – 2, 3 or 4?
604. In which year was Tom born in Nottingham – 1984, 1985 or 1986?
605. Which Spurs manager signed Tom for the club?
606. What is Tom's middle name – Andrew, Aaron or Anthony?
607. Against which club did Tom score Tottenham's second goal in a 2-0 home League win during November 2009?
608. True or false: Tom scored the club's only goal in a 1-0 home League win against Bolton Wanderers during May 2010?
609. Against which team did Tom score a brace for Spurs, in the 80th and 99th minutes, in a 3-1 home win (after extra time) in the League Cup 4th round during November 2006?
610. True or false: Tom scored twice for Tottenham, both times in the UEFA Cup, during the 2008/09 season?

DAVID HOWELLS
611. How many League goals did David score for Spurs in the first Premier League season, during 1992/93?
612. In which year was David born in Guildford – 1965, 1967 or 1969?
613. True or false: David scored on his Tottenham League debut, in a 2-1 win at Sheffield Wednesday during February 1986?
614. How many League games did David play for Spurs in his playing career - 277, 287 or 297?
615. What nationality is David – Welsh, Scottish or English?

616. How many League goals did David score for Tottenham in his playing career – 18, 20 or 22?
617. For which club did David sign when he left The Lane in 1998?
618. In what position did David play during his playing days?
619. David scored for Spurs against which two teams during the 1996/97 season?
620. Which Spurs manager handed David his Tottenham League debut?

FA CUP WINNERS - 1981
621. Which Spurs midfielder scored a brace for Spurs in a 3-2 win in the FA Cup final replay?
622. Which team did Spurs beat in the FA Cup final replay?
623. Which player for the opposition scored for his own team and also scored Spurs' equaliser in the 79th minute in the FA Cup final?
624. Can you name Spurs' goalkeeper in the FA Cup final and FA Cup final replay?
625. Which Tottenham manager guided the club to this success?
626. What was the name of Tottenham's Cup final song, recorded by the musical duo Chas and Dave?
627. Can you name seven of Tottenham's starting eleven in the FA Cup final replay?
628. True or false: the year of 1981 marked the 100th FA Cup final in history?
629. What was the score at half-time in the FA Cup final replay, with the game finishing 3-2 to Tottenham?
630. Was this the 5th, 6th or 7th time that Spurs had won the FA Cup in their history?

2000/2001
631. Which defender did Spurs purchase from Wimbledon for £5 million during July 2000?
632. How many League goals did Sergei Rebrov score during this season, his first season at The Lane?
633. Ian Walker played in goal three games this season, but which goalkeeper played in the other 35 League games?

634. Which Tottenham midfielder scored the club's winner in the 41st minute in a 2-1 home win against Liverpool during November 2000?

635. Which team did Tottenham beat 3-0 at home, with Steffen Iversen, Les Ferdinand and Sergei Rebrov scoring the goals, during March 2001?

636. Which Tottenham defender scored a brace, including an 88th-minute winner, away at Sunderland in a 3-2 win during April 2001?

637. Which Dutch midfielder scored a Tottenham brace in a 3-1 home win against Manchester United during May 2001?

638. Which East Anglian team did Spurs beat 3-1 at home on the opening day of the League season during August 2000?

639. How many of their 19 away League games did Tottenham win – 2, 10 or 18?

640. Which forward finished as Tottenham's top League scorer this season, with ten goals?

LEAGUE HAT-TRICKS

Match up the League opponents with the player who scored a hat-trick for Spurs

641. v. Leeds United, February 1993	Jermain Defoe
642. v. Everton, December 1998	Jermain Defoe
643. v. Everton, January 2003	Teddy Sheringham
644. v. Wigan Athletic, November 2009	Les Ferdinand
645. v. Sunderland, March 1997	Jürgen Klinsmann
646. v. Wimbledon, May 1998	Teddy Sheringham
647. v. Southampton, December 2004	Robbie Keane
648. v. Leicester City, November 2000	Jermain Defoe
649. v. Hull City, August 2009	Chris Armstrong

650. v. Newcastle United,
December 1994   Steffen Iversen

TIM SHERWOOD

651. How many League goals did Tim score for Spurs in his football career – 10, 12 or 14?
652. From which team did Tim sign when he arrived at White Hart Lane in 1999?
653. Against which team did Tim make his Spurs League debut, in a 0-0 home draw during February 1999?
654. True or false: Tim made his full England debut at the age of 35?
655. In which year was Tim born in St Albans – 1967, 1968 or 1969?
656. Against which team did Tim score a Spurs brace in a 4-0 home League win on Boxing Day 1999?
657. In what position did Tim play during his playing days - left back, central midfielder or striker?
658. Against which team did Tim score Spurs' second and winning goal in a 2-1 home League win during November 1999?
659. Which Spurs manager signed Tim for Tottenham in 1999?
660. How many League appearances did Tim make for Spurs in his career - 93, 153 or 193?

1999/2000

661. Which team did Spurs beat 7-2 at home during March 2000?
662. Following on from the previous question, which Spurs striker scored a hat-trick in the game?
663. Which forward scored the club's only goal in a 1-0 home win against Liverpool during January 2000?
664. What was the score when Sunderland visited White Hart Lane in May 2000, the last day of the League season?
665. Which team did Spurs beat 3-1 at home during August 1999, with Steffen Iversen, Les Ferdinand and Tim Sherwood scoring the goals?
666. Who was Spurs' boss during this season?
667. Can you name the two Spurs strikers that finished the season with 14 League goals?

668. Who was the only Tottenham player to play in all 38 League matches this season?

669. How many of their 38 League matches did the club win during this season – 15, 17 or 19?

670. True or false: Spurs were unbeaten in the four League matches played in January 2000?

JERMAINE JENAS

671. From which club did Jermaine sign when he joined Spurs in August 2005?

672. Against which club did Jermaine make his Spurs debut, in a 0-0 home League draw in September 2005?

673. Against which club did Jermaine score his first Tottenham League goal, in a 2-0 home win during October 2005?

674. What is Jermaine's middle name – Anthony, Adrian or Arthur?

675. Against which country did Jermaine score his first England international goal, in a 2-1 England win during February 2008?

676. How many League goals did Jermaine score for Tottenham in his first season at the club, during the 2005/06 season?

677. Against which team did Jermaine score his only League goal of the 2009/10 season, in a 5-0 home win during September 2009?

678. In which year was Jermaine born in Nottingham – 1981, 1982 or 1983?

679. Against which Midlands team did Jermaine score Spurs' only goal in a 1-0 home League win during May 2009?

680. At which club did Jermaine start his professional football career?

KEITH BURKINSHAW

681. How many times did Keith guide Spurs to win the FA Cup during his managerial career?

682. True or false: Keith played for Spurs during his playing career?

683. Although he is known by the name Keith, this is his middle name. What is his real first name?

684. In which year did Keith leave The Lane, with Peter Shreeves taking over as Spurs' boss?

685. What was the last Cup that Spurs won whilst Keith was the Tottenham manager?
686. In which position did Keith play during his playing days – defender, midfielder or striker?
687. Which English team did Keith manage during the 1993/94 season?
688. In which year was Keith born in Barnsley – 1933, 1935 or 1937?
689. Who was Tottenham's manager before Keith took charge at The Lane in 1976?
690. True or false: Keith is Tottenham's second most successful manager in the club's history behind Bill Nicholson?

ROBBIE KEANE

691. Against which London team did Robbie make his Spurs debut, in a 3-2 home win during September 2002, with Simon Davies, Teddy Sheringham and Anthony Gardner scoring Tottenham's goals?
692. Against which team did Robbie score a Tottenham hat-trick in a 4-3 home League win during January 2003?
693. Against which team did Robbie score a Spurs brace in a 4-1 home League win during February 2007, with Jermaine Jenas and Aaron Lennon scoring the other goals?
694. Against which team did Robbie score four goals for Spurs in a 5-0 home win in the Premier League during September 2009?
695. How many League goals did Robbie score for Tottenham during the 2005/06 season – 14, 16 or 18?
696. For which country is Robbie a full international?
697. For which Italian team did Robbie play during the 2000/01 season?
698. For which team did Robbie sign when he left The Lane in 2008, only to return to Tottenham in 2009?
699. Which Tottenham manager signed Robbie for his first spell at the club?
700. In which year was Robbie born in Dublin – 1978, 1979 or 1980?

JUANDE RAMOS

701. Which team did Spurs beat 2-0 in the League Cup 4th round in Juande's first match in charge at Tottenham during October 2007?
702. Following on from the previous question, can you name the two Spurs scorers in the game?
703. How many of their 54 League matches did the club win under Juande – 18, 21 or 24?
704. True or false: Juande retired from playing football at the age of 28 due to a knee injury?
705. Which Spanish team did Juande manage before he was appointed as Spurs' boss?
706. To which position did Juande guide Tottenham in the Premier League during the 2007/08 season – 9th,10th or 11th?
707. In which year was Juande born – 1953, 1954 or 1955?
708. In what position did Juande play during his playing days?
709. Which Cup did Juande win as Spurs' manager during his time at the club?
710. Which Spanish giants did Juande go on to manage when he left Spurs, during the 2008/09 season?

1998/1999

711. How many of their League matches did the club win during this season – 11, 13 or 15?
712. Which defender left The Lane for Aston Villa during March 1999?
713. Which striker scored nine League goals, finishing as Tottenham's highest League scorer this season?
714. Which forward scored the only goal in Spurs' third League match and first League win of the season, a 1-0 away win against Everton during August 1998?
715. What was the score when Tottenham visited Charlton Athletic during April 1999?
716. Can you name Spurs' two goalscorers in a 2-2 home draw with Chelsea in the League during May 1999?
717. Which defender scored Tottenham's 90th-minute equaliser in a 3-3 home League draw against Leeds United during September 1998?
718. Who started the season as Tottenham manager?

719. Which defender scored a brace, including Tottenham's 90th-minute equaliser, in a 2-2 home League draw against Manchester United during December 1998?

720. Which defender signed for Spurs from Ipswich Town during November 1998?

LEDLEY KING

721. What is Ledley's middle name – Brenton, Brendan or Breedon?

722. Which squad number did Ledley wear during the 2010/11 season?

723. Against which country did Ledley play for England for 45 minutes in their first game of the 2010 World Cup, the game ending in a 1-1 draw, with Steven Gerrard scoring England's goal?

724. Which manager handed Ledley his Tottenham League debut in 1999?

725. Against which team did Ledley score his first goal for Tottenham, in a 3-3 draw during December 2000, setting a new Premier League record for the quickest goal scored in a game at just 10.2 seconds?

726. Against which team did Ledley make his League debut for Spurs, in a 3-2 away defeat during May 1999?

727. In what position does Ledley play?

728. True or false: Ledley won the Premier League Player of the Month award during September 2004?

729. Against which country did Ledley score for England in a 3-1 win at Wembley in a friendly match during May 2010?

730. In which year was Ledley born in London – 1979, 1980 or 1981?

AARON LENNON

731. From which club did Aaron sign for Spurs in 2005?

732. True or false: Aaron won Tottenham's Player of the Year and Young Player of the Year awards at the end of the 2008/09 season?

733. How many League goals did Aaron score for Spurs during the 2008/09 season – 3, 5 or 7?

734. Against which London team did Aaron make his Spurs debut, in a 2-0 home defeat during August 2005?

735. Against which Midlands team did Aaron score his first Spurs goal, in a 2-0 away League win during March 2006?
736. Against which two countries did Aaron play for England in the 2010 World Cup in South Africa?
737. What squad number did Aaron wear for Spurs during the 2010/11 season?
738. What was the transfer free when Aaron joined Tottenham?
739. What is Aaron's middle name – Jamie, Justin or Jonathan?
740. Against which London team did Aaron score Tottenham's winner in the 52nd minute in a 2-1 home League win during November 2006?

1997/1998
741. Can you name the three Spurs goalscorers in Tottenham's 3-3 League home draw against Liverpool during March 1998?
742. Which Spurs midfielder scored in the 28th minute against Arsenal in a 1-1 League draw at The Lane during December 1997?
743. Which Italian midfielder did Tottenham sign from Inter Milan during January 1998?
744. True or false: Spurs were unbeaten in the five League matches played during April 1998?
745. Against which club did Spurs record their first League win of the season, during August 1997, with Colin Calderwood scoring the only goal in the game, after defeats to Manchester United (at home) and West Ham United (away)?
746. In which position did Spurs finish in the League – 12th, 14th or 16th?
747. Which Tottenham striker finished as the club's highest League scorer with 9 goals in 15 matches?
748. Who started the season as Spurs' boss before Christian Gross took charge in November 1997?
749. Which winger did Spurs sign from Sporting Lisbon during August 1997?
750. Which striker scored Tottenham's only goal in a 1-0 home League win against West Ham United during January 1998?

GARY LINEKER

751. How many League goals did Gary score for Tottenham in his career – 65, 66 or 67?
752. In what year did Gary sign for Spurs from Barcelona?
753. True or false: Gary scored 28 League goals in 35 matches for Spurs during the 1991/92 season?
754. Against which country did Gary score his first England hat-trick, in a World Cup qualifier 5-0 win at Wembley Stadium during October 1985?
755. Where in England was Gary born in 1960 – Leeds, Leicester or London?
756. For which English team did Gary play during the 1985/86 season, finishing the season with 30 League goals, his best ever tally in a League season in his professional career?
757. How many goals did Gary score for England in his career – 47, 48 or 49?
758. What is Gary's middle name – Winston, Wilfred or William?
759. In how many League games did Gary play for Spurs in his football career – 85, 95 or 105?
760. For which Japanese team did Gary sign when he left The Lane in 1992?

GARY MABBUTT

761. How many League goals did Gary score for Tottenham in his career, in 458 starts and 19 substitute appearances – 23, 25 or 27?
762. In what year did Gary make his final Spurs appearance, in a 1-1 home League draw against Southampton?
763. Against which team did Gary score Tottenham's winning goal in a 2-1 home win in the Premier League during December 1992?
764. True or false: Gary scored for both sides in the Spurs v. Coventry City FA Cup final in 1987, which ended in a 3-2 Tottenham defeat?
765. Can you recall the name of either Gary's father or his brother, both former professional footballers?
766. From which club did Gary sign for Spurs in 1982?
767. What trophy did Gary lift as Spurs captain in 1991?

768. How many full international England caps did Gary win during his playing career, scoring one goal for his country – 15, 16 or 17?
769. In what position did Gary play during his playing days?
770. In which year was Gary born in Bristol – 1961, 1963 or 1965?

NAYIM
771. From which Spanish team did Spurs sign Nayim in the late 1980s?
772. How many League games did Nayim play for Spurs in his football career – 102, 112 or 122?
773. Which Spurs manager sign Nayim for Tottenham?
774. Against which East Anglian team did Nayim score Spurs' fifth goal in a 5-1 home League win during April 1993?
775. In what position did Nayim play – defender, midfielder or striker?
776. True or false: Nayim represented Spain at under 18, under 19, under 20 and under 21 level?
777. Against which club did Nayim score a Spurs hat-trick in a 4-2 FA Cup away win in 1993?
778. How many League goals did Nayim score for Spurs in his football career – 9, 11 or 13?
779. Which winners' medal did Nayim pick up during his time at Tottenham?
780. For which Spanish team did Nayim sign in 1993 when he left White Hart Lane?

GEORGE GRAHAM
781. George was in charge at which club in between his management spells at Arsenal and Tottenham?
782. Which Cup did George win for Tottenham in his first season in charge at White Hart Lane?
783. In which year was George born in Glasgow – 1942, 1943 or 1944?
784. To what position in the League did George guide Spurs during his first season in charge?
785. Which striker did George sign for Spurs from Dynamo Kiev during June 2000?
786. Which midfielder did George sign from Blackburn Rovers for £4 million during February 1999?

787. What percentage of games did George win as Spurs manager – 39%, 42% or 45%?
788. To what position in the League did George guide Spurs during the 1999/2000 season?
789. For which country did George win 12 international caps, scoring 3 goals, in his career?
790. In what year was George sacked as Tottenham manager?

1996/1997

791. How many League goals did Teddy Sheringham score for Spurs during this season – 7, 8 or 9?
792. Goalkeeper Ian Walker started 37 of Spurs' 38 League matches this season, but who took his place in goal in the game he missed?
793. Which team did Tottenham beat 3-1 at The Lane on Boxing Day 1996, with Steffen Iversen scoring a brace and Allan Nielsen scoring the other Spurs goal?
794. True or false: Tottenham were unbeaten in their three League matches played during February 1997?
795. Which Tottenham striker scored a hat-trick away at Sunderland in a 4-0 League win during March 1997?
796. Who managed Spurs during this season, his last full season in charge at The Lane?
797. How many of their 38 League matches did the club win during this season - 13, 14 or 15?
798. Which defender signed for Spurs from Liverpool during December 1996?
799. Can you name the only Spurs player to play in all 38 League matches during this season?
800. Which team beat Spurs 7-1 away from home during December 1996?

ROMAN PAVLYUCHENKO

801. What nationality is Roman?
802. How many League goals did Roman score for Spurs in his first season at The Lane, during the 2008/09 season?
803. Against which team did Roman make his Spurs debut, in a 2-1 home defeat during September 2008?

804. Against which team did Roman score a brace in a 4-0 home win in an FA Cup 5th round replay during February 2010?
805. What squad number did Roman wear during the 2010/11 season?
806. In what position does Roman play?
807. Against which team did Roman score his first Spurs goal, in the 62nd minute of a 2-1 away win in the League Cup 3rd round during September 2008?
808. Against which Lancashire team did Roman score a Spurs League brace in a 3-1 home win during March 2010, with Jermain Defoe scoring the other Tottenham goal?
809. In which year was Roman born – 1980, 1981 or 1982?
810. From which Russian team did Roman sign for Spurs in 2008?

FA CUP WINNERS - 1982
811. Which goalkeeper played in both the FA Cup final and FA Cup final replay for Spurs?
812. What was the score in the FA Cup final replay, after drawing the final 1-1 at Wembley?
813. Which London team did Spurs beat in the FA Cup final replay?
814. Can you name the three non-English players that played for Spurs in the FA Cup final and FA Cup final replay?
815. Which team did Spurs beat in the FA Cup semi-final?
816. Was this victory Spurs' 7th, 8th or 9th FA Cup win in their history?
817. True or false: Spurs went into the FA Cup final as holders of the trophy?
818. Who was Tottenham's captain during this success?
819. Which Tottenham player scored in both the FA Cup final and FA Cup final replay?
820. Which Spurs manager guided the club to this success?

STEVE PERRYMAN
821. In which year was Steve born in London - 1951, 1953 or 1955?
822. Against which team did Steve make his Spurs debut, in a 1-0 defeat at home during September 1969?

823. How many League goals did Steve score for Spurs during the 1980/81 season – 2, 4 or 6?
824. How old was Steve when he became Spurs' captain?
825. How many times did Steve win the FA Cup whilst a Spurs player?
826. How many League appearances did Steve make for Spurs during his playing career - 655, 705 or 755?
827. For which team did Steve sign when he left White Hart Lane in 1986?
828. Against which country did Steve win his only full England cap, as a substitute during June 1982?
829. In what year did Steve win the Football Writers' Association Footballer of the Year award?
830. How many League goals did Steve score for Tottenham in his football career - 31, 41 or 51?

1995/1996

831. Can you name two of the three Spurs goalscorers in the club's 3-2 away League win against Coventry City during November 1995?
832. Which Tottenham striker scored the club's winner in a 2-1 home League win against Arsenal during November 1995?
833. Which team finished higher in the League – Tottenham or Chelsea?
834. What was the score when Tottenham visited Southampton at The Dell on Boxing Day 1995?
835. How many of their 38 League matches did the club win - 16, 17 or 18?
836. Which Spurs striker scored a brace in the club's 4-1 home League win against Manchester United on New Year's Day 1996?
837. Who was Spurs' boss during this season?
838. Which midfielder left White Hart Lane for Reading during February 1996?
839. Against which team did Spurs record their first League win of the season, a 2-1 home win in their fifth League game during September 1995?
840. Which Spurs player scored a brace in a 3-1 away League win against Leeds United during May 1996?

GUS POYET
841. From which London team did Gus sign when he came to The Lane in 2001?
842. In what position did Gus play - defender, midfielder or striker?
843. For which country was Gus a full international during his playing days?
844. How many League appearances did Gus make for Tottenham in his football career – 80, 82 or 84?
845. Which Spurs manager signed Gus in June 2001?
846. Against which team did Gus score a brace for Spurs in a 4-0 home win in the FA Cup 5th round during February 2002?
847. For which Spanish team did Gus play between 1990 and 1997?
848. Against which team did Gus score Tottenham's winner, in the 89th minute, in a 4-3 home League win during February 2004?
849. Gus became manager of which English club in 2009?
850. How many League goals did Gus score for Tottenham in his career – 16, 18 or 20?

MARTIN JOL
851. In what year was Martin appointed as Spurs manager?
852. When Martin first arrived at White Hart Lane he took up the position of assistant to which Spurs manager?
853. True or false: Martin won the Manager of the Month award in only his second month in charge of Tottenham?
854. In which year was Martin born in The Netherlands – 1956, 1957 or 1958?
855. To what position did Martin guide Spurs during the 2006/07 season, securing UEFA Cup qualification on the final day of the season and making him the first Spurs manager since Keith Burkinshaw to qualify for European football in successive seasons?
856. In which position did Martin play during his playing days – defender, midfielder or striker?
857. For which two English teams did Martin play during his playing days, the first from 1982 to 1984 and the second from 1984 to 1985?

858. Martin was appointed as manager of which Dutch side in 2009?
859. Who took over from Martin as boss at The Lane during October 2007?
860. True or false: Martin was a full international for his country during his playing days?

1994/1995

861. Which team did Spurs beat 4-3 away from home on the opening day of the League season, with Darren Anderton, Nick Barmby, Jürgen Klinsmann and Teddy Sheringham scoring the goals for Tottenham during August 1994?
862. Who started the season as Tottenham manager?
863. Which midfielder did Tottenham purchase from PSV Eindhoven for £2.9 million during September 1994?
864. Can you name Tottenham's two goalscorers in the 2-0 away win against Norwich City on Boxing Day 1994?
865. What was the score when Tottenham played Coventry City away from home on New Year's Eve 1994?
866. Which striker scored Tottenham's goal at Highbury when Spurs and Arsenal drew 1-1 in the League during April 1995?
867. Which team finished highest in the League – Tottenham, Chelsea or Arsenal?
868. Which Tottenham defender left White Hart Lane for Bolton Wanderers during March 1995?
869. Which forward scored a League hat-trick for Spurs in a 4-2 home win over Newcastle United during December 1994?
870. Which team beat Spurs 4-3 at White Hart Lane during November 1994, in Gerry Francis's first League game in charge at the club?

GRAHAM ROBERTS

871. How many League appearances did Graham make for Tottenham during his Spurs career - 209, 309 or 409?
872. True or false: Graham won full international caps for England during his playing career?
873. Can you name the three winners' medals that Graham won whilst a Spurs player?

874. For which London team did Graham play between 1988 and 1990?
875. In what position did Graham play during his playing days?
876. What is Graham's middle name – Paul, Peter or Philip?
877. What is the name of Graham's 2008 autobiography?
878. For which team did Graham sign when he left White Hart Lane in 1986?
879. How many League goals did Graham score for Spurs in his career – 13, 23 or 33?
880. Against which team did Graham make his Tottenham League debut, in a 3-2 away win during October 1980?

1993/1994

881. Which Spurs striker scored the only goal on the opening day of the League season, in a 1-0 away win against Newcastle United?
882. Can you name the Spurs League goalscorers in a 3-3 home draw against Liverpool during December 1993?
883. How many of their 42 League matches did the club win - 11, 13 or 15?
884. Which striker did Tottenham sign from Liverpool during January 1994?
885. Which team did Spurs beat 5-0 at home in the League during September 1993, with Teddy Sheringham scoring a brace in the game?
886. True or false: Spurs lost all four League matches during January 1994?
887. Which fullback signed for Tottenham from Leeds United during September 1993?
888. Which team did Spurs beat 3-0 at home in the League during April 1994, with Darren Anderton, Vinny Samways and Steve Sedgley scoring the goals?
889. Can you name Tottenham's two scorers in a 2-2 away League draw with Sheffield United during September 1993?
890. Which striker left White Hart Lane for Rangers during November 1993?

PAUL ROBINSON

891. How many League appearances did Paul make for Spurs in his career – 127, 137 or 147?

892. In what year did Paul join Tottenham?
893. From which Yorkshire team did Paul sign when he arrived at The Lane?
894. Against which team did Paul score Tottenham's second goal in the 63rd minute of a 3-1 home League win during March 2007?
895. What was the only winners' medal that Paul won at Tottenham during his career?
896. How many full international caps did Paul win for England during his playing career – 21, 31 or 41?
897. True or false: Paul was ever present in League competition for Spurs during the 2005/06 and 2006/07 seasons?
898. How many League goals did Paul score for Tottenham in his career - 1, 2 or 3?
899. What is Paul's middle name – William, Wayne or Warren?
900. For which club did Paul sign when he left White Hart Lane in 2008?

VINNY SAMWAYS

901. How many League appearances did Vinny make for Tottenham in his playing career - 193, 195 or 197?
902. For which Premier League team did Vinny sign when he left The Lane in 1994?
903. True or false: Vinny was in Tottenham's starting eleven in the 1991 FA Cup final against Nottingham Forest?
904. In what position did Vinny play during his playing days?
905. How many League goals did Vinny score for Spurs in the 1988/89 season - 3, 5 or 7?
906. True or false: Vinny won a full international cap for England during his playing days?
907. Against which team did Vinny make his Spurs debut, in a 2-1 defeat away during May 1987?
908. In which year was Vinny born in London – 1967, 1968 or 1969?
909. For which Midlands team did Vinny play during the 2003/04 season?
910. How many League goals did Vinny score for Tottenham during his career – 11, 13 or 15?

DAVID PLEAT

911. In which 1980s season did David manage Spurs?
912. What is David's middle name – John, Joseph or James?
913. To what position in the League did David guide Tottenham during his season as manager?
914. True or false: David guided Tottenham to both the FA Cup final and the League Cup semi-finals during his season in charge of the club?
915. Which team did David manage from 1978, prior to taking charge at Tottenham?
916. In what year did David return to White Hart Lane as Director of Football?
917. True or false: David once played a League match for Tottenham during his playing days?
918. In what position did David play during his playing days?
919. Which team did David manage between 1995 and 1997?
920. In which year was David born in Nottingham – 1943, 1945 or 1947?

SQUAD NUMBERS – 2010/2011

Match up the player with the squad number they wore during the 2010/2011 season

921.	Kyle Walker	8
922.	Younes Kaboul	25
923.	Wilson Palacios	39
924.	Roman Pavlyuchenko	1
925.	Heurelho Gomes	12
926.	Sébastien Bassong	4
927.	Danny Rose	28
928.	David Bentley	9
929.	Jonathan Woodgate	5
930.	Jermaine Jenas	19

WHITE HART LANE

931. Tottenham's ground, White Hart Lane, is situated on the High Road in Tottenham, but can you recall the postcode?
932. Against which team did Spurs play their first game, a friendly, at White Hart Lane, in a 4-1 win in front of a crowd of 5,000?

933. In what year was the South Stand redeveloped, including the installation of the first giant Sony Jumbotron TV screen at the ground?

934. True or false: White Hart Lane hosted American football in 1995 and 1996 as the home ground of the London Monarchs?

935. What is the nearest tube station to White Hart Lane, a 1.4 mile walk to the stadium?

936. Against which team did Spurs achieve their record home attendance of 75,038, in an FA Cup tie during March 1938?

937. In which year did the club move to White Hart Lane – 1899, 1900 or 1901?

938. Which stand is situated on Bill Nicholson Way?

939. What are the dimensions of Tottenham's pitch – 95 metres x 62 metres, 100 metres x 67 metres or 105 metres x 72 metres?

940. What is the name of the train station that is situated about a four-minute walk away from the stadium?

CLUB HISTORY

941. In what year was the club formed?

942. Which Dutch player signed for Spurs in August 2010 from Real Madrid?

943. Which club did Spurs play in their first ever Champions League match, in the play-off first leg at White Hart Lane during August 2010, in a 3-2 away defeat?

944. Can you name the three teams who were in Tottenham's group (group A) in the Champions League during the 2010/2011 season?

945. In what year did Spurs first win the FA Cup?

946. Who scored a hat-trick for Spurs in the Champions League play-off second leg in a 4-0 home win during August 2010?

947. When Spurs won the League Cup in 2008, was this the 2nd, 3rd or 4th time the club had won this trophy in their history?

948. Which team did Tottenham beat 9-0, to record their record League win, playing in the Second Division during October 1977?

949. Which French defender signed for Spurs from Arsenal during August 2010?
950. Who were the club's first ever shirt sponsors in their history?

LEAGUE APPEARANCES – 3

Match up the player with the number of League appearances he made for Spurs in his career

951.	Timothée Atouba	91 (1)
952.	Young-Pyo Lee	10 (11)
953.	Micky Hazard	22 (1)
954.	Mark Bowen	17 (4)
955.	Paul Gascoigne	60
956.	Rory Allen	68 (2)
957.	Chris Fairclough	23 (10)
958.	Hossam Ghaly	88 (31)
959.	Espen Baardsen	14 (3)
960.	Andy Gray	15 (3)

SQUAD NUMBERS – 1994/1995

Match up the player with the squad number he wore during the 1994/95 season

961.	Gheorghe Popescu	14
962.	Ian Walker	15
963.	Sol Campbell	3
964.	Ronny Rosenthal	7
965.	Justin Edinburgh	22
966.	Ilie Dumitrescu	13
967.	David Howells	8
968.	David Kerslake	4
969.	Nick Barmby	11
970.	Stuart Nethercott	23

LEAGUE APPEARANCES – 4

Match up the player with the number of League appearances he made for Spurs in his career

971.	Gerry Armstrong	12 (10)
972.	Dean Austin	28 (3)
973.	Matthew Etherington	61 (3)
974.	Ian Crook	152 (11)
975.	Ray Clemence	11 (4)

976. Michael Carrick	20 (25)
977. Colin Calderwood	65 (19)
978. Stéphane Dalmat	240
979. Edgar Davids	10 (10)
980. Sean Davis	117 (7)

POSITIONS IN THE LEAGUE

Match up the season with the club's finishing position in Division One

981.	1980/81	13th in Division One
982.	1981/82	3rd in Division One
983.	1982/83	3rd in Division One
984.	1983/84	10th in Division One
985.	1984/85	10th in Division One
986.	1985/86	3rd in Division One
987.	1986/87	8th in Division One
988.	1987/88	4th in Division One
989.	1988/89	4th in Division One
990.	1989/90	6th in Division One

INTERNATIONALS

Match up the player with the number of caps he won for his country during his football career

991.	Steve Archibald	5 Caps for England
992.	Jamie Redknapp	53 Caps for Republic of Ireland
993.	Kasey Keller	9 Caps for Nigeria
994.	Anthony Gardner	27 Caps for Scotland
995.	Ronny Rosenthal	36 Caps for Scotland
996.	Gordon Durie	17 Caps for England
997.	John Chiedozie	43 Caps for Scotland
998.	Chris Hughton	60 Caps for Israel
999.	Paul Walsh	102 Caps for USA
1000.	Colin Calderwood	1 Cap for England

2012/2013 - THE LEAGUE SEASON

1001. Against which team did Tottenham record their first League win of the 2012/2013 season, winning 3-1 away from home during September 2012?

1002. When Spurs were winning 2-1 against Arsenal at White Hart Lane during March 2013, at the end of the 90 minutes how much stoppage time did the fourth official show there was to play, which caused so much tension amongst Spurs fans – 2 minutes, 4 minutes or 6 minutes?

1003. Can you name the two Spurs players that hit the bar during the 3-1 home League win against West Ham United during November 2012?

1004. Against which team did Sandro score a League goal, in Tottenham's 3-0 away win during December 2012?

1005. Which Spurs defender scored Tottenham's goal in the 2-1 away defeat to Manchester City during November 2012?

1006. How many League goals did Emmanuel Adebayor score for Spurs during the 2012/2013 season?

1007. True or false: Not one player was ever-present for Spurs in their 38 League matches during the 2012/2013 season?

1008. Against which team did Benoit Assou-Ekotto score his only Spurs League goal of the 2012/2013 season, in a 1-1 draw during August 2012?

1009. Which Spurs defender scored his first home League goal for four years when he equalised for Spurs against Reading on New Year's Day 2013, Spurs went on to win the match 3-1?

1010. Which company appeared on the front of Tottenham's shirts in all League games during the 2012/2013 season?

1011. Against which London club did Tottenham beat 2-1 at White Hart Lane, to record Andre Villas-Boas' first win at home during September 2012?

1012. Which Spurs player scored on his 400th League appearance in his career, scoring a goal for Spurs on Boxing Day 2012 in a 4-0 away win at Aston Villa?

1013. In which position in the League were Spurs at the end of November 2012 – 1st, 3rd or 5th?

1014. Which team visited The Lane in December 2012 and were beaten 1-0 by a Jan Vertonghen goal and failed to record a single shot on target during the 90 minutes?

1015. Which Tottenham defender won the 'Premier League Player of the Month' award during March 2013?

1016. True or false: Aaron Lennon scored four goals for Spurs during the 2012/2013 season, and Spurs won all four League matches?

1017. When Tottenham visited the Britannia Stadium during the 2012/2013 season which club did they play?

1018. Against which club did Tottenham share a 1-1 League draw at White Hart Lane during January 2013, in very snowy conditions, with Clint Dempsey grabbing the Spurs goal?

1019. Which Spurs striker scored Tottenham's winning goal eight minutes from the end of the match in the 2-1 away win at Stoke City during May 2013?

1020. Against which club did Tottenham record their biggest attendance of the 2012/2013 season, with a crowd of 36,763?

1021. Which Tottenham midfielder scored the second goal for Spurs in the club's 2-1 home win over The Gooners during March 2013?

1022. True or false: Tottenham won their last League match of 2012?

1023. Which Spurs midfielder scored Tottenham's goal in the 1-1 home draw against Norwich City during August 2012 on his League debut for the club?

1024. How many League goals did Jermain Defoe score for Spurs during the 2012/2013 season – 9, 10 or 11?

1025. True or false: Lewis Holtby scored a League goal for Spurs during the 2012/2013 season?

1026. Against which club did Gareth Bale score his 20th League goal of the 2012/2013 season, in a 1-0 home win at the start of May 2013?

1027. Can you name the two Spurs players that scored the goals for Tottenham in the 2-2 away draw at Stamford Bridge when the club played Chelsea in the Premier League during May 2013?

1028. True or false: Jermain Defoe scored a League hat-trick for Spurs during the 2012/2013 season?

1029. In which position in the League were Spurs at the end of March 2013?

1030. Spurs finished joint sixth in the 2012/2013 fair play League with which club, receiving 54 yellow cards and 2 red cards during the season?

1031. Which Spurs player scored a brace in the 3-2 away defeat to Liverpool during March 2013?

1032. True or false: Tottenham failed to score more than four goals in a League game during the 2012/2013 season?

1033. Which team was former boss Harry Redknapp managing when Andre Villas-Boas took Spurs away from home during January 2013, and the two teams shared a 0-0 draw?

1034. In which position in the Premier League did Tottenham finish at the end of the 2012/2013 season – 4th, 5th or 6th?

1035. How many League goals did Gylfi Sigurdsson score for Spurs during the 2012/2013 season – 3, 6 or 9?

1036. Can you name the teams that finished above Tottenham in the 2012/2013 League season?

1037. Arsenal beat Spurs 5-2 at The Emirates Stadium but which Spurs striker was sent-off whilst Spurs were winning 1-0?

1038. Which former Spurs boss was managing Fulham when he brought them to White Hart Lane in March 2013 and beat Spurs 1-0 in the League?

1039. True or false: Tottenham were unbeaten in League competition in their last eight matches of the 2012/2013 season?

1040. With how many points did Tottenham end the 2012/2013 League season – 70, 71 or 72?

2012/2013 - THE BOSS - ANDRE VILLAS-BOAS

1041. Which Tottenham manager did Andre replace at White Hart Lane?

1042. True or false: Andre lost his first Spurs League match?

1043. Can you name the two months that Andre won the 'Premier League Manager of the Month' award during the 2012/2013 season whilst managing Tottenham Hotspur?

1044. Which English team did Andre manage before being appointed Spurs boss?

1045. How old was Andre when he took charge at The Lane – 33, 34 or 35?

1046. Who was the Tottenham chairman who appointed Andre as manager during the summer of 2012?

1047. How many of Tottenham's 38 League matches did Andre guide Spurs to victory?

1048. In which month during 2012 was Andre appointed Spurs boss?

1049. Andre became the first Spurs manager to win at which club for 23 years when Tottenham won 3-2 away in the Premier League during September 2012?

1050. What nationality is Andre?

2012/2013 - STAR PLAYER - GARETH BALE

1051. How many League goals did Gareth score for Spurs during the 2012/2013 season in his 33 League appearances?

1052. Against which London team did Gareth score a Tottenham brace in a 3-2 away win in the League during February 2013?

1053. Against which team did Gareth score Tottenham's only goal on the last day of the League season, during May 2013 with Spurs winning 1-0?

1054. In which year was Gareth born in Cardiff – 1988, 1989 or 1990?

1055. Against which club did Gareth score a League hat-trick for Tottenham in a 4-0 away win during December 2012?

1056. During which month of the 2012/2013 season did Gareth win the 'Premier League Player of the Month' award?

1057. What is Gareth's middle name – Martin, Chris or Frank?

1058. How many Europa League goals did Gareth score for Spurs during the 2012/2013 season, in his 8 Europa League appearances?

1059. From which club did Tottenham sign Gareth in 2007?

1060. How tall is Gareth – 5 foot 10 inches, 5 foot 11 inches or 6 foot?

2012/2013 - SQUAD NUMBERS

Match the player with the squad number he wore during the 2012/2013 season

1061. Gareth Bale	25
1062. Jermain Defoe	2
1063. Andros Townsend	7
1064. Clint Dempsey	11
1065. Jan Vertonghen	18
1066. Hugo Lloris	6
1067. Aaron Lennon	5
1068. Brad Friedel	22
1069. Gylfi Sigurdsson	24

1070. Tom Huddlestone   31

2012/2013 - TRANSFERS
Match the player with the team he signed from/for during the 2012/2013 season

1071. Lewis Holtby   Signed for Mallorca from Spurs
1072. Luka Modric   Signed for Spurs from Fulham
1073. Jan Vertonghen   Signed for Queens Park Rangers from Spurs
1074. Rafael van der Vaart   Signed for Everton from Spurs
1075. Hugo Lloris   Signed for Spurs from Fulham
1076. Giovani Dos Santos   Signed for Spurs from Ajax
1077. Clint Dempsey   Signed for Spurs from Lyon
1078. Jermaine Jenas   Signed for Spurs from Schalke 04
1079. Mousa Dembele   Signed for Real Madrid from Spurs
1080. Steven Pienaar   Signed for Hamburg from Spurs

2012/2013 - TRIVIA – POT LUCK
1081. Which team did Spurs beat 3-0 at White Hart Lane in the FA Cup third round during January 2013?
1082. Which Tottenham striker scored a brace at home in the FA Cup third round?
1083. True or false: Spurs signed three players from Millwall during the 2012/2013 season?
1084. Did assistant manager Steffen Freund sit to AVB's right or left during matches?
1085. Which team knocked Spurs out of the FA Cup, during the fourth round tie during January 2013, Spurs losing 2-1, with Clint Dempsey scoring a header for Tottenham?
1086. Which company appeared on the front of Tottenham's shirts in all cup competitions during the 2012/2013 season?
1087. Which squad number did Kyle Walker wear during the 2012/2013 season – 2, 12 or 28?
1088. Which team did Spurs beat 3-0 in the League Cup third round during September 2012?
1089. How much was a match day programme at White Hart Lane during the 2012/2013 season?

1090. Which Spurs player scored Tottenham's goal in the 2-1 defeat away at Norwich City in the League Cup fourth round during October 2012?

2012/2013 - THE EUROPA LEAGUE
1091. In which Europa League group were Spurs, with Lazio, NK Maribor and Panathinaikos – Group H, Group I or Group J?
1092. What was the score when Lazio visited The Lane during September 2012, in the Europa League?
1093. Which Spurs striker scored his first ever competitive goal at White Hart Lane in the 3-1 home win against Panathinaikos in the Europa League?
1094. True or false: When Jermain Defoe scored his second goal of his hat-trick in the 3-1 home win against NK Maribor during November 2012, it was Tottenham's 200th goal in UEFA Cup/Europa League competition?
1095. Which Italian side did Spurs beat 3-0 at home in the first leg of the last 16 in the competition?
1096. True or false: Spurs were unbeaten in all 6 Europa League group matches?
1097. What was the score when Spurs played FC Basel in the quarter-final first leg at White Hart Lane during April 2013?
1098. Who scored both goals for Tottenham in the 2-2 away draw at FC Basel in the quarter-final second leg during April 2013?
1099. Which Belgian defender was sent-off for Spurs when they played FC Basel away in the quarter-final second leg during April 2013?
1100. Spurs lost on penalties to FC Basel after extra time in the quarter-final of the competition, which two players missed Tottenham's penalties?

2013/2014 - THE LEAGUE SEASON
1101. In which position in the Premier League did Spurs finish at the end of the 2013/2014 season?
1102. In which month during the 2013/2014 season did Andre Villas-Boas leave White Hart Lane?
1103. With how many points did Tottenham finish the 2013/2014 Premier League season – 67, 68 or 69?

1104. Who was Tottenham's top League scorer during the 2013/2014 season?

1105. In which position in the Premier League were Spurs after the first six games?

1106. Which Spurs striker scored a brace in the 4-0 away win at Newcastle United during February 2014?

1107. True or false: Spurs lost 1-0 to Arsenal at home and away during the 2013/2014 season?

1108. Which Tottenham played scored the only goal from the penalty spot in a 1-0 home win against Hull City during October 2013?

1109. What was the score when Southampton visited The Lane on Sunday 23 March 2014 in the Premier League?

1110. With which club did Spurs share a 3-3 away draw in the Premier League during April 2014, having been 3-0 down after 31 minutes?

1111. Which London team did Tottenham beat 2-1 away during December 2013 with Lewis Holtby grabbing the winner in the 82nd minute?

1112. How many League goals did Harry Kane score for Spurs during the 2013/2014 season?

1113. True or false: Tottenham beat Swansea City 3-1 away during January 2014?

1114. What was the attendance at White Hart Lane when Arsenal visited in March 2014 – 34,711, 35,711 or 36,711?

1115. Which London club beat Spurs 2-0 in the Premier League during May 2014?

1116. In how many of the clubs 38 Premier League matches did Hugo Lloris play?

1117. Which Tottenham midfielder scored the winning goal in stoppage time away at Cardiff City during September 2013?

1118. Which Spurs midfielder made his League debut for the club when he came on in the 83rd minute against Aston Villa in the club's 3-0 home win during May 2014?

1119. Which Spurs defender scored Tottenham's third goal in the 3-1 home win against Fulham during April 2014?

1120. How many League goals did Christian Eriksen score for Tottenham during the 2013/2014 season?

1121. Can you name the defender that made his Spurs League debut in the 5-1 home win against Sunderland, wearing the number 51 shirt?

1122. True or false: Liverpool beat Tottenham 5-0 at White Hart Lane in the Premier League during December 2013?

1123. Against which club did Jermain Defoe score his final Tottenham goal during January 2014 in a 2-0 home win?

1124. Which Spurs player scored Tottenham's second goal in the 2-1 away win against Manchester United on New Year's Day 2014?

1125. Against which Premier League team did Vlad Chiriches score his only League goal of the season, in a 2-1 away win during December 2013?

1126. Which London team beat Spurs 3-0 at The Lane during October 2013?

1127. How many League goals did Paulinho score for Spurs during the 2013/2014 season?

1128. Who scored Tottenham's first goal after 31 minutes at Villa Park in a 2-0 win during October 2013?

1129. Which team did Spurs beat 3-0 at White Hart Lane on the last day of the League season?

1130. Can you name the two Tottenham goal scorers when Spurs drew 2-2 with Manchester United at White Hart Lane in December 2013?

1131. Which Spurs midfielder scored a brace against Southampton at home during March 2014?

1132. Which team did Spurs play at home on Monday 7 April 2014 in the League?

1133. What was the score when Tottenham recorded their heaviest defeat of the 2013/2014 season away at Manchester City during November 2013?

1134. Which referee took charge of the Tottenham home match to Everton during February 2014?

1135. Which team visited The Lane on Boxing Day 2013 and shared a 1-1 draw with Spurs?

1136. Can you name the Spurs defender who scored the clubs only goal in the 1-0 away win at Stoke City during April 2014?

1137. With which team did Tottenham share a 0-0 away draw on 3 November 2013?

1138. True or false: The 2013/2014 season was Tottenham's 22nd Premier League season?
1139. Which London club did Tottenham beat 1-0 away on the opening day of the Premier League season during August 2013?
1140. Which company was advertised on the front of Tottenham's home shirts during the 2013/2014 Premier League season?

2013/2014 - THE BOSS – TIM SHERWOOD
1141. In which year did Tim play his final competitive match for Spurs?
1142. When Tim was appointed Spurs coach in October 2008 who was Tottenham's manager?
1143. True or false: Under Tim's management Spurs were unbeaten in the Premier League in his first six matches in charge at the club?
1144. In which year was Tim born in St. Albans – 1967, 1969 or 1971?
1145. Against which club did Tottenham record a 3-2 away win in the Premier League during December 2013, this being Tim's first League match as Spurs boss?
1146. How many caps did Tim win for England during his playing career?
1147. True or false: Whilst growing up Tim was an Arsenal fan and his dad still is?
1148. Which Arsenal defender did Tim throw the ball at as he wanted him to hurry up and take the throw-in during the club's 1-0 home defeat during March 2014?
1149. For which team did Tim sign when he left White Hart Lane?
1150. True or false: Tim did not shake hands with Benfica manager Jorge Jesus after the club's 3-1 home defeat in the Europa League during March 2014?

2013/2014 STAR PLAYER – EMMANUEL ADEBAYOR
1151. Which squad number did Emmanuel wear during the 2013/2014 season?
1152. Was the 2013/2014 season Emmanuel's first, second or third season at White Hart Lane?

1153. How many League appearances did Emmanuel make for Spurs during the 2013/2014 season – 20, 21 or 22?

1154. Against which London team did Emmanuel score in the League Cup fifth round during December 2013?

1155. True or false: Emmanuel scored one of the goals in Tottenham's 3-0 Premier League win against Stoke City during December 2013?

1156. In which minute of the game did Emmanuel score against Aston Villa on the last day of the League season when Spurs won 3-0 at White Hart Lane – 28th, 38th or 48th?

1157. True or false: Emmanuel did not play a League match under the management of Andre Villas-Boas during the 2013/2014 season?

1158. How tall is Emmanuel – 6 foot 2 inches, 6 foot 3 inches or 6 foot 4 inches?

1159. Which Spurs striker finished the season as Emmanuel's strike partner?

1160. True or false: Emmanuel was sent-off in Tottenham's home match against Arsenal during March 2014?

2013/2014 - SQUAD NUMBERS
Match the player with the squad number he wore during the 2013/2014 season

1161. Harry Kane	5
1162. Andros Townsend	16
1163. Danny Rose	42
1164. Jan Vertonghen	2
1165. Aaron Lennon	3
1166. Christian Eriksen	25
1167. Kyle Naughton	37
1168. Hugo Lloris	7
1169. Nabil Bentaleb	23
1170. Kyle Walker	17

2013/2014 - TRANSFERS
1171. From which Dutch team did Spurs sign Christian Eriksen in August 2013?

1172. For which Canadian team did Jermain Defoe sign when he left The Lane at the end of February 2014?

1173. Which Spurs midfielder signed for Hull City in August 2013 for £5 million?

1174. How much did Tottenham pay for Roberto Soldado in the summer of 2013?

1175. Which Argentinean player did Spurs purchase in August 2013?

1176. To which Spanish club did Tottenham sell Gareth Bale on 1 September 2013?

1177. Which London club signed Scott Parker when he left The Lane in August 2013?

1178. From which Dutch team did Tottenham sign Nacer Chadli in July 2013?

1179. How much did Tottenham pay Brazilian team Corinthians for midfielder Paulinho in July 2013?

1180. Which Tottenham midfielder signed for Millwall on 31 January 2014 on loan until the end of the season?

2013/2014 - TRIVIA – POT LUCK

1181. How much was a match day programme at White Hart Lane during the 2013/2014 season?

1182. True or false: Spurs issued the squad number 60 to a member of Tottenham's squad during the 2013/2014 season?

1183. Which team knocked Spurs out of the FA Cup in the third round during January 2014, beating Tottenham 2-0?

1184. True or false: Spurs did not concede a single goal in any competitive match they played during August 2013?

1185. Which Spurs midfielder made his 100th competitive appearance for Tottenham in the 4-0 away defeat at Chelsea during March 2014?

1186. What nationality is Etienne Capoue?

1187. In which position did Michael Dawson play during the 2013/2014 season?

1188. Which company were Tottenham's shirt sponsors in all cup competitions (FA Cup, League Cup and the Europa League) during the 2013/2014 season?

1189. Which former German Spurs player was assistant manager to Tim Sherwood during the 2013/2014 season?

1190. True or false: Tottenham reached the League Cup final during the 2013/2014 season?

2013/2014 - THE EUROPA LEAGUE
1191. Against which Portuguese team did Spurs lose 3-1 at White Hart Lane during the first leg, round of 16 during the 2013/2014 season?
1192. Which team did Tottenham beat 3-2 on aggregate in the round of 32 during the 2013/2014 season?
1193. Which Spurs striker scored a hat-trick in the home match against FC Anji in the 4-1 win during the 2013/2014 season?
1194. What time did all of Tottenham's home matches in the Europa League kick-off during the 2013/2014 season?
1195. True or false: Spurs won all eight Europa League games under the management of Andre Villas-Boas during the 2013/2014 season?
1196. Against which team did Jan Vertonghen score in the 2-0 Europa League away win during October 2013?
1197. What was the attendance at White Hart Lane when Benfica visited in the round of 16 during March 2014 – 33,283, 34,283 or 35,283?
1198. Which Tottenham striker scored a brace in the club's 3-1 home win against Dnipro in the round of 32 second leg during February 2014?
1199. True or false: Hugo Lloris scored a Europa League goal for Spurs during the 2013/2014 season?
1200. Which Spurs player scored a brace against Benfica in the 2-2 away draw during March 2014 in the round of 16 second leg?

2014/2015 - THE BOSS - MAURICIO POCHETTINO
1201. In which month during 2014 was Mauricio appointed Tottenham manager?
1202. Which English club did Mauricio manage before managing Spurs?
1203. In which year was Mauricio born – 1970, 1971 or 1972?
1204. In which position did Mauricio play during his playing days?
1205. Which Spanish team did Mauricio manage between 2009 and 2012?
1206. How tall is Mauricio – 5 foot, 10 inches, 5 foot 11 inches or 6 foot?
1207. What nationality is Mauricio?

1208. Which London club did Tottenham beat 1-0 on the opening day of the 2014/2015 season; this being Mauricio's first competitive match in charge of the club?
1209. True or false: Tottenham won the first four competitive matches of the 2014/2015 season, with Mauricio in charge at White Hart Lane?
1210. How many full international caps did Mauricio achieve in his football career as a player?

2014/2015 - SQUAD NUMBERS
Match the player with the squad number he wore during the 2013/2014 season

1211. Benjamin Stambouli	8
1212. Harry Kane	38
1213. Hugo Lloris	21
1214. Erik Lamela	1
1215. Ryan Mason	6
1216. Federico Fazio	15
1217. Michael Vorm	11
1218. Paulinho	18
1219. Eric Dier	13
1220. Vlad Chiriches	25

2014/2015 - NEW SIGNINGS
1221. Which Spurs defender made his League debut on the opening day of the Premier League season during August 2014 and scored the only goal in a 1-0 away win?
1222. From which club did Tottenham sign Ben Davies during July 2014?
1223. On which date did Spurs sign defender Federico Fazio – 19 August 2014, 23 August 2014 or 27 August 2014?
1224. Can you name the midfielder that Spurs signed from Montpellier on 1 September 2014?
1225. From which club did Tottenham sign Eric Dier during August 2014?
1226. Which Dutch goalkeeper arrived at White Hart Lane from Swansea City on 23 July 2014?
1227. In which position does Michel Vorm play?
1228. From which club did Tottenham sign Federico Fazio during August 2014?

1229. In which year was Ben Davies born – 1991, 1992 or 1993?
1230. True or false: Eric Dier scored on his League debut away from home, and then scored in the next League match on his home debut?

2014/2015 - POT LUCK
1231. Who was named as Mauricio Pochettino's assistant manager in May 2014?
1232. Which Cyprus based team did Tottenham beat in the UEFA Europa Qualifiers, 2-1 away and 3-0 at home, making it an aggregate score of 5-1?
1233. With which German team did Spurs play a friendly at White Hart Lane on 9 August 2014, with Tottenham winning 2-1?
1234. True or false: Tottenham signed a 17-year-old striker called Harry Cowlin from Arsenal during August 2014?
1235. Which Premier League team were the first to beat Tottenham in the 2014/2015 season?
1236. True or false: After the first two Premier League matches Spurs were top of the League?
1237. Can you name the Spurs goalkeeper who played in all five competitive matches during August 2014?
1238. With which Premier League team did Tottenham share a 2-2 away draw on 13 September 2014?
1239. How much was a match-day programme at White Hart Lane during the 2014/2015 season?
1240. Which London team did Spurs beat 4-0 at White Hart Lane in the Premier League during August 2014?

2014/2015 - NATIONALITIES
Match up the Tottenham Hotspur player with his nationality

1241. Michel Vorm	English
1242. Ben Davies	French
1243. Erik Lamela	English
1244. Eric Dier	Dutch
1245. Kyle Walker	Welsh
1246. Federico Fazio	French
1247. Brad Friedel	Argentinean
1248. Hugo Lloris	American
1249. Benjamin Stambouli	English
1250. Harry Kane	Argentinean

ANSWERS:

JÜRGEN KLINSMANN
1.	Ossie Ardiles
2.	20
3.	Sheffield Wednesday
4.	Everton
5.	Sampdoria
6.	Teddy Sheringham
7.	1964
8.	29
9.	Bayern Munich
10.	2004

HARRY REDKNAPP
11.	False: he never played a League game for Spurs
12.	2008
13.	Juande Ramos
14.	League Cup final
15.	Bolton Wanderers
16.	Daniel Levy
17.	Peter Crouch
18.	West Ham United
19.	1947
20.	8th

2009/2010
21.	Liverpool
22.	Jermain Defoe
23.	Burnley
24.	5
25.	Fulham
26.	Luka Modrić and Jermain Defoe
27.	Roman Pavlyuchenko
28.	Sébastien Bassong
29.	Sunderland
30.	Peter Crouch

HONOURS
31.	FA Cup Winners	1991
32.	Charity Shield Winners (joint)	1982
33.	League Cup Winners	1999
34.	Charity Shield Winners (joint)	1992
35.	FA Cup Winners	1981
36.	Peace Cup (Korea) Winners	2005
37.	League Cup Winners	2008

38.	FA Youth Cup Winners	1990
39.	FA Cup Winners	1982
40.	UEFA Cup Winners	1984

LEGENDS - 1
41. Glenn Hoddle
42. Teddy Sheringham
43. Ossie Ardiles
44. Ricky Villa
45. David Ginola
46. Gary Mabbutt
47. Jermain Defoe
48. Ray Clemence
49. Garth Crooks
50. Ian Walker

FA CUP WINNERS – 1991
51. Nottingham Forest
52. Erik Thorstvedt
53. 2-1 to Spurs (after extra time)
54. Stuart Pearce
55. Nayim and Paul Walsh
56. Mark Crossley
57. Erik Thorstvedt, Pat van den Hauwe, Gary Mabbutt, Steve Sedgley, Justin Edinburgh, David Howells, Paul Gascoigne, Paul Stewart, Paul Allen, Gary Lineker and Vinny Samways
58. Des Walker
59. Terry Venables
60. Arsenal

MANAGERS
61.	Terry Venables	1987
62.	Gerry Francis	1994
63.	George Graham	1998
64.	Glenn Hoddle	2001
65.	Martin Jol	2004
66.	Christian Gross	1997
67.	Doug Livermore	1992
68.	Juande Ramos	2007
69.	David Pleat	1986
70.	Ossie Ardiles	1993

FIRST PREMIER LEAGUE SEASON – 1992/1993
71. Southampton
72. True: a 2-0 win at home against Sheffield United
73. John Hendry
74. 16

75.	Teddy Sheringham
76.	Leeds United
77.	Southampton
78.	Gordon Durie
79.	8th
80.	Teddy Sheringham

LEAGUE GOALS – 1
81.	Chris Armstrong	48
82.	Darren Anderton	34
83.	Paul Allen	23
84.	Nico Claesen	18
85.	Sol Campbell	10
86.	Guy Butters	1
87.	Darren Bent	18
88.	Dimitar Berbatov	27
89.	Nick Barmby	20
90.	Clive Allen	60

WHERE DID THEY COME FROM? – 1
91.	Niko Kranjčar	Portsmouth
92.	Carlo Cudicini	Chelsea
93.	David Bentley	Blackburn Rovers
94.	Aaron Lennon	Leeds United
95.	Danny Murphy	Charlton Athletic
96.	Edgar Davids	Inter Milan
97.	Gareth Bale	Southampton
98.	Darren Bent	Charlton Athletic
99.	Chris Gunter	Cardiff City
100.	Heurelho Gomes	PSV Eindhoven

JERMAIN DEFOE
101.	Colin
102.	West Ham United
103.	18
104.	Portsmouth
105.	Portsmouth
106.	West Ham United
107.	Portsmouth
108.	Leeds United
109.	13
110.	Holland

TEDDY SHERINGHAM
111.	Sheffield United
112.	1 (against Leeds United at home in a 4-0 win during February 1993)
113.	Manchester United
114.	Millwall (1984-91) and West Ham United (2004-07)

115. 18
116. 1966
117. Newcastle United
118. 236: 230 (6)
119. Glenn Hoddle
120. 97

2008/2009
121. Aaron Lennon
122. 4-4
123. Roman Pavlyuchenko
124. Juande Ramos
125. Pascal Chimbonda
126. Darren Bent
127. Liverpool
128. Carlo Cudicini
129. Roman Pavlyuchenko
130. 8th

OSSIE ARDILES
131. 16
132. Escape to Victory
133. Nottingham Forest
134. Blackburn Rovers, Queens Park Rangers and Swindon Town
135. True
136. 5
137. FA Cup (1981 and 1982) and UEFA Cup (1984)
138. 238: 222 (16)
139. 1993
140. Argentinian

LES FERDINAND
141. 17
142. Fulham
143. Bolton Wanderers
144. Gerry Francis
145. West Ham United
146. Striker
147. 33
148. Aston Villa
149. League Cup (1999)
150. Newcastle United

2007/2008
151. 11th
152. Robbie Keane and Dimitar Berbatov
153. Chelsea
154. Dimitar Berbatov

155. Gilberto
156. 1-1
157. Dimitar Berbatov
158. Robbie Keane and Tom Huddlestone
159. Jonathan Woodgate
160. Younes Kaboul

LEAGUE APPEARANCES - 1
161. David Tuttle   10 (3)
162. Terry Yorath   44 (4)
163. Sergei Rebrov   37 (22)
164. David Kerslake   34 (3)
165. Kazuyuki Toda   2 (2)
166. Luke Young   44 (14)
167. Andy Reid   20 (6)
168. Ian Walker   257 (2)
169. Neil Ruddock   45 (2)
170. Teemu Tainio   48 (13)

POT LUCK – 1
171. Spurs or Lilywhites
172. 2001
173. 'To Dare is To Do'
174. Hewlett Packard
175. 2 (1981 and 1982)
176. 1971, 1973, 1999 and 2008
177. Jacques Santini (took over in 2004)
178. Michael Dawson
179. North
180. 2005/06

CHRIS ARMSTRONG
181. 48
182. Crystal Palace
183. True: away against Everton during October 1995
184. Manchester United
185. 1971
186. Blackburn Rovers
187. 2
188. Wrexham
189. Liverpool
190. Gerry Francis

LEAGUE APPEARANCES - 2
191. Dean Richards   73
192. Jamie Redknapp   37 (11)
193. Garry Brady   0 (9)
194. Gary Lineker   105

195.	Erik Edman	31
196.	Moussa Saïb	3 (10)
197.	Kevin Scott	16 (2)
198.	John Scales	29 (4)
199.	Johnnie Jackson	12 (8)
200.	Øyvind Leonhardsen	46 (8)

LEGENDS – 2
201. Paul Allen
202. Robbie Keane
203. Ledley King
204. Joe Kinnear
205. Steve Perryman
206. Gary Lineker
207. Paul Gascoigne
208. Clive Allen
209. Chris Hughton
210. David Howells

POT LUCK - 2
211. True
212. Ossie Ardiles (appointed manager in 1993)
213. Swiss
214. Thomson Holidays
215. True
216. Aaron Lennon
217. 2007
218. £11 million
219. 1884
220. Admiral

CLIVE ALLEN
221. True
222. Queens Park Rangers
223. 1961
224. Les Allen
225. 105: 97 (8)
226. Darren
227. Everton
228. Peter Shreeves
229. 60
230. Bordeaux

WHERE DID THEY COME FROM? – 2
231.	Steve Hodge	Aston Villa
232.	Richard Gough	Dundee United
233.	Bobby Mimms	Everton
234.	Paul Walsh	Liverpool

235.	Steve Sedgley	Coventry City
236.	Justin Edinburgh	Southend United
237.	Pat Van Den Hauwe	Everton
238.	Teddy Sheringham	Nottingham Forest
239.	Clive Wilson	Queens Park Rangers
240.	Gica Popescu	PSV Eindhoven

GARETH BALE
241. Wales
242. 3
243. Southampton
244. Arsenal, Chelsea and Burnley
245. Fulham
246. 1989
247. 2 (during the 2007/08 season)
248. Football League Young Player of the Year award and Football Association of Wales Young Player of the Year award
249. Frank
250. True

LEAGUE GOALS – 2
251.	Simon Davies	13
252.	Stephen Kelly	2
253.	Micky Hazard	15
254.	Tony Galvin	20
255.	Gary Doherty	4
256.	Terry Fenwick	8
257.	Mark Falco	68
258.	Ilie Dumitrescu	4
259.	Ruel Fox	13
260.	Jason Dozzell	13

2006/2007
261. 5th
262. Ricardo Rocha
263. Dimitar Berbatov
264. Michael Dawson and Aaron Lennon
265. Charlton Athletic
266. Robbie Keane
267. Jermaine Jenas
268. Paul Stalteri
269. Aston Villa
270. Paul Robinson

DIMITAR BERBATOV
271. Bulgaria
272. Bayer Leverkusen
273. Sheffield United

274. Fulham
275. 4
276. 1981
277. True
278. 27
279. 2008
280. £10.9 million

DAVID GINOLA
281. 13
282. Aston Villa
283. PFA Players' Player of the Year and Football Writers' Player of the Year
284. League Cup (1999)
285. 1967
286. True
287. Newcastle United
288. Carlisle United
289. 100
290. Barnsley

2005/2006
291. True: 2-0 win against Portsmouth (away), 2-0 win against Middlesbrough (home) and 0-0 draw against Blackburn Rovers (away)
292. Blackburn Rovers
293. Robbie Keane
294. Paul Robinson
295. 16
296. 5th
297. Aaron Lennon
298. Michael Carrick
299. Martin Jol
300. Robbie Keane

SPURS IN THE FA CUP
301. 1901, 1921, 1961, 1962, 1967, 1981, 1982 and 1991
302. Arsenal
303. 6-1 to Newcastle United
304. 5th round (during March 1986)
305. Everton
306. Nayim
307. West Ham United
308. Robbie Keane
309. Manchester United
310. 1987 (against Coventry City)

LEAGUE GOALS – 3
311.	Dean Marney	2
312.	Steed Malbranque	6
313.	Mbulelo Mabizela	1
314.	Steve Perryman	31
315.	Noé Pamarot	1
316.	Noureddine Naybet	1
317.	Nayim	11
318.	John Moncur	1
319.	Mido	1
320.	Pedro Mendes	13

WHERE DID THEY GO? – 1
321.	Kevin Boateng	Portsmouth
322.	Gordon Durie	Rangers
323.	John Polston	Norwich City
324.	Paul Walsh	Portsmouth
325.	Paul Stewart	Liverpool
326.	John Moncur	Swindon Town
327.	Phil Gray	Luton Town
328.	Richard Gough	Rangers
329.	Chris Gunter	Nottingham Forest
330.	Ian Crook	Norwich City

LEAGUE GOALS – 4
331.	Andy Reid	1
332.	Graham Roberts	23
333.	Ronny Rosenthal	4
334.	Neil Ruddock	3
335.	Paul Stewart	28
336.	Paul Stalteri	2
337.	Andy Turner	3
338.	Ramon Vega	7
339.	Ricardo Villa	18
340.	Mauricio Taricco	2

SPURS IN THE LEAGUE CUP
341. 1971, 1973, 1999 and 2008
342. 5-1 to Spurs
343. Chris Armstrong
344. Sol Campbell
345. Southend United
346. Hartlepool United
347. Vinny Samways
348. Oldham Athletic
349. 5-1 to Spurs
350. 1982

WHERE DID THEY COME FROM? – 3

351.	John Scales	Liverpool
352.	Ramon Vega	Cagliari
353.	José Dominguez	Sporting Lisbon
354.	Nicola Berti	Inter Milan
355.	Mauricio Taricco	Ipswich Town
356.	Anthony Gardner	Port Vale
357.	Gary Doherty	Luton Town
358.	Neil Sullivan	Wimbledon
359.	Chris Perry	Wimbledon
360.	Øyvind Leonhardsen	Liverpool

LEAGUE CUP FINALISTS - 2009

361. Manchester United
362. 0-0
363. 88,217
364. Ben Foster (Manchester United's goalkeeper)
365. Michael Dawson and Ledley King
366. Jamie O'Hara, Gareth Bale and David Bentley
367. Harry Redknapp
368. 5 (Michael Dawson, Ledley King, Aaron Lennon, Jermaine Jenas and Darren Bent)
369. March (1 March 2009)
370. Burnley (Spurs won 4-1 at home and lost 3-2 away)

WHERE DID THEY GO? – 2

371.	Gudni Bergsson	Bolton Wanderers
372.	Gica Popescu	Barcelona
373.	Kevin Scott	Norwich City
374.	Dean Austin	Crystal Palace
375.	Ronny Rosenthal	Watford
376.	Clive Wilson	Cambridge United
377.	Jason Cundy	Ipswich Town
378.	Steve Slade	Queens Park Rangers
379.	Darren Caskey	Reading
380.	Vinny Samways	Everton

LEAGUE CUP WINNERS - 2008

381. Chelsea
382. Juande Ramos
383. Paul Robinson
384. 1-1 (with Spurs scoring in extra time to win 2-1)
385. Dimitar Berbatov
386. Pascal Chimbonda and Steed Malbranque
387. True
388. Mark Halsey
389. True
390. Jonathan Woodgate (in the 94th minute)

WHERE DID THEY GO? – 3

391.	Ramon Vega	Watford
392.	Milenko Ačimovič	Lille
393.	Chris Perry	Charlton Athletic
394.	Gary Doherty	Norwich City
395.	Steffen Iversen	Wolves
396.	Stephen Clemence	Birmingham City
397.	Ben Thatcher	Leicester City
398.	Jamie Redknapp	Southampton
399.	Neil Sullivan	Chelsea
400.	Alton Thelwell	Hull City

TERRY VENABLES

401. 5
402. True
403. 13th
404. Bill Nicholson
405. 115: 114 (1)
406. Chelsea
407. El Tel
408. England
409. FA Cup winners' medal in 1967
410. 1943

2004/2005

411. Frederic Kanoute (2), Ledley King and Stephen Kelly
412. 2-0 to Tottenham
413. Dean Marney
414. Liverpool
415. Michael Dawson
416. Jermain Defoe (13) and Robbie Keane (11)
417. Radek Černý (he also made 1 substitute appearance against Aston Villa during May 2005)
418. 14
419. Michael Carrick
420. Jermain Defoe

GARTH CROOKS

421. True
422. FA Cup winners' medals in 1981 and 1982 and UEFA Cup medal in 1984
423. Anthony
424. 1980
425. 16 (during the 1980/81 season)
426. Nottingham Forest (during August 1980)
427. Forward
428. 48
429. True

430. West Bromwich Albion

LEAGUE CUP WINNERS - 1999
431. Leicester City
432. Allan Nielsen
433. George Graham
434. 5 (Ian Walker, Sol Campbell, Justin Edinburgh, Darren Anderton and Les Ferdinand)
435. Steffen Freund
436. March (21 March 2009)
437. Worthington Cup
438. 77,892
439. Ramon Vega
440. Wimbledon (0-0 draw at home and 1-0 away win)

DARREN ANDERTON
441. Portsmouth
442. 6
443. League Cup (1999)
444. 299: 273 (26)
445. Southampton
446. Leeds United
447. Southampton
448. False: he scored 26
449. Robert
450. 7

MARK FALCO
451. 174: 162 (12)
452. Keith Burkinshaw
453. 22
454. True
455. Striker
456. 1960
457. 68
458. Bolton Wanderers
459. UEFA Cup winner in 1984
460. Watford

PAUL STEWART
461. Blackpool
462. True: in the 53rd minute
463. Manchester City
464. 28
465. Terry Venables
466. Manchester United
467. Andrew
468. 131: 126 (5)

469. True: he won 3 full international caps during his football career
470. Liverpool

PETER SHREEVES
471. True
472. 1940
473. 3rd (during the 1984/85 season)
474. David Pleat
475. 1991/92
476. False: he never played for Spurs
477. Chelsea
478. False: he has never managed England
479. Inside forward
480. 2 (1984-86 and 1991-92)

PAUL GASCOIGNE
481. 19
482. Newcastle United
483. 1992
484. True
485. 6
486. FA Cup winners' medal in 1991
487. Kettering Town
488. 92: 91(1)
489. John
490. Midfielder

2003/2004
491. Robbie Keane
492. Leicester City
493. Wolves
494. 13
495. David Pleat
496. Gus Poyet
497. 14
498. Kasey Keller
499. Michael Brown
500. Stéphane Dalmat

RICKY VILLA
501. 18
502. 1952
503. FA Cup winners' medals in 1981 and 1982
504. Central midfielder
505. Keith Burkinshaw
506. Argentinian
507. 1978
508. 1981/82

509. Nottingham Forest
510. 133: 124 (9)

CHRIS WADDLE
511. 33
512. Sheffield Wednesday
513. 1960
514. Marseille
515. 6
516. Roland
517. Watford
518. 138: 137 (1)
519. Newcastle United
520. 14

PAUL WALSH
521. 1962
522. Manchester United
523. Liverpool
524. 19
525. False: he was an Arsenal fan
526. FA Cup winner in 1991
527. Striker
528. True: he won 5 caps, scoring 1 goal
529. Portsmouth
530. 128: 84 (44)

CHRISTIAN ZIEGE
531. German
532. 2001
533. True
534. 7
535. Arsenal
536. Middlesbrough
537. 5 (during the 2001/02 season)
538. True: Tottenham equaliser after 33 minutes
539. Glenn Hoddle
540. 47: 44 (3)

2002/2003
541. Robbie Keane
542. True: Spurs lost 5-1 away to Middlesbrough and 4-0 at home to Blackburn Rovers
543. 2-0 to Tottenham (Teddy Sheringham and Robbie Keane scoring the goals)
544. Charlton Athletic
545. Robbie Keane (13 goals) and Teddy Sheringham (12 goals)
546. Kasey Keller

547. 5
548. Gus Poyet
549. Charlton Athletic (12th), Fulham (14th) and West Ham United (18th)
550. Robbie Keane

UEFA CUP WINNERS - 1984
551. Paul Miller
552. Tony Parks, Danny Thomas, Chris Hughton, Graham Roberts, Paul Miller, Gary Mabbutt, Micky Hazard, Gary Stevens, Tony Galvin, Steve Archibald and Mark Falco
553. Keith Burkinshaw
554. Graham Roberts
555. May 1984
556. 46,258
557. Hajduk Split
558. Steve Archibald and Mark Falco
559. Graham Roberts, Mark Falco, Gary Stevens and Steve Archibald
560. Graham Roberts

GERRY FRANCIS
561. 1994 (19 November was the day of his first match against Aston Villa)
562. 10th
563. David Ginola
564. Bristol Rovers
565. Christian Gross
566. False: he never played for Spurs during his playing career
567. 1951
568. Queens Park Rangers
569. Semi-finals, then losing 4-1 at Elland Road against Everton
570. 7th (during the 1994/95 season)

GLENN HODDLE
571. 88
572. 2001
573. 'Diamond Lights'
574. 377: 370 (7)
575. Terry Neill
576. AS Monaco
577. True
578. 2 (1981 and 1982)
579. 1957
580. England

CHRIS HUGHTON
581. Fullback
582. 53
583. 2 (1981 and 1982)

584.   3
585.   West Ham United
586.   Newcastle United
587.   12
588.   Manchester City
589.   1958
590.   297: 293 (4)

2001/2002
591.   Dean Richards
592.   Gus Poyet and Teddy Sheringham
593.   Neil Sullivan
594.   Gus Poyet
595.   14
596.   Kasey Keller
597.   Glenn Hoddle
598.   Gus Poyet
599.   Manchester United
600.   9

TOM HUDDLESTONE
601.   Derby County
602.   Fabio Capello
603.   3
604.   1986
605.   Martin Jol
606.   Andrew
607.   Sunderland
608.   True
609.   Port Vale
610.   True: against Dynamo Zagreb (in a 4-0 home win during November 2008) and against Spartak Moscow (in a 2-2 home draw during December 2008)

DAVID HOWELLS
611.   1 (against Blackburn Rovers in a 2-0 away win during November 1992)
612.   1967
613.   True
614.   277: 238 (39)
615.   English
616.   22
617.   Southampton
618.   Midfielder
619.   Chelsea (at home in a 2-1 defeat during February 1997) and West Ham United (away in a 4-3 defeat during February 1997)
620.   Peter Shreeves

FA CUP WINNERS - 1981
621. Ricky Villa
622. Manchester City
623. Tommy Hutchison
624. Milija Aleksic
625. Keith Burkinshaw
626. 'Ossie's Dream'
627. Milija Aleksic, Chris Hughton, Paul Miller, Graham Roberts, Ricky Villa, Steve Perryman, Ossie Ardiles, Steve Archibald, Tony Galvin, Glenn Hoddle and Garth Crooks
628. True
629. 1-1
630. 6th

2000/2001
631. Ben Thatcher
632. 9
633. Neil Sullivan
634. Tim Sherwood
635. Coventry City
636. Gary Doherty
637. Willem Korsten
638. Ipswich Town
639. 2
640. Les Ferdinand

LEAGUE HAT-TRICKS
641. v. Leeds United, February 1993 — Teddy Sheringham
642. v. Everton, December 1998 — Chris Armstrong
643. v. Everton, January 2003 — Robbie Keane
644. v. Wigan Athletic, November 2009 — Jermain Defoe
645. v. Sunderland, March 1997 — Steffen Iversen
646. v. Wimbledon, May 1998 — Jürgen Klinsmann
647. v. Southampton, December 2004 — Jermain Defoe
648. v. Leicester City, November 2000 — Les Ferdinand
649. v. Hull City, August 2009 — Jermain Defoe
650. v. Newcastle United, December 1994 — Teddy Sheringham

TIM SHERWOOD
651. 12
652. Blackburn Rovers
653. Coventry City
654. False: he was 30 when he made his full debut in England's 3-1 victory over Poland at Wembley during March 1999
655. 1969
656. Watford
657. Central midfielder
658. Arsenal

659. George Graham
660. 93: 81 (12)

1999/2000
661. Southampton
662. Steffen Iversen
663. Chris Armstrong
664. 3-1 to Tottenham
665. Newcastle United
666. George Graham
667. Steffen Iversen and Chris Armstrong
668. Ian Walker
669. 15
670. False: won 1, drew 1 and lost 2

JERMAINE JENAS
671. Newcastle United
672. Liverpool
673. Everton
674. Anthony
675. Switzerland
676. 6
677. Burnley
678. 1983
679. West Bromwich Albion
680. Nottingham Forest

KEITH BURKINSHAW
681. 2 (1981 and 1982)
682. False: he never played for Spurs in his playing days
683. Harry
684. 1984
685. UEFA Cup (1984)
686. Defender
687. West Bromwich Albion
688. 1935
689. Terry Neill
690. True

ROBBIE KEANE
691. West Ham United
692. Everton
693. Bolton Wanderers
694. Burnley
695. 16
696. Republic of Ireland
697. Inter Milan
698. Liverpool

699. Glenn Hoddle (in 2002)
700. 1980

JUANDE RAMOS
701. Blackpool
702. Robbie Keane and Pascal Chimbonda
703. 21
704. True
705. Sevilla
706. 11th
707. 1954
708. Midfielder
709. League Cup (2008)
710. Real Madrid

1998/1999
711. 11 (7 at home and 4 away)
712. Colin Calderwood
713. Steffen Iversen
714. Les Ferdinand
715. 4-1 to Tottenham
716. Steffen Iversen and David Ginola
717. Sol Campbell
718. Christian Gross
719. Sol Campbell
720. Mauricio Taricco

LEDLEY KING
721. Brenton
722. 26
723. USA
724. George Graham
725. Bradford City
726. Liverpool
727. Central defender
728. True
729. Mexico
730. 1980

AARON LENNON
731. Leeds United
732. True
733. 5
734. Chelsea
735. Birmingham City
736. USA and Algeria
737. 7
738. £1 million

739. Justin
740. Chelsea

1997/1998
741. Jürgen Klinsmann, David Ginola and Ramon Vega
742. Allan Nielsen
743. Nicola Berti
744. False: won 1, drew 3 and lost 1
745. Derby County
746. 14th
747. Jürgen Klinsmann
748. Gerry Francis
749. José Dominguez
750. Jürgen Klinsmann

GARY LINEKER
751. 67
752. 1989
753. True
754. Turkey
755. Leicester
756. Everton (his only season playing for Everton)
757. 48
758. Winston
759. 105
760. Nagoya Grampus Eight

GARY MABBUTT
761. 27
762. 1998
763. Nottingham Forest
764. True: he scored for Tottenham in the 40th minute and for Coventry in the 96th minute
765. Ray Mabbutt (father) and Kevin Mabbutt (brother)
766. Bristol Rovers
767. FA Cup
768. 16
769. Centre back
770. 1961

NAYIM
771. Barcelona
772. 112: 95 (17)
773. Terry Venables
774. Norwich City
775. Midfielder
776. True
777. Manchester City

778. 11
779. FA Cup (1991)
780. Real Zaragoza

GEORGE GRAHAM
781. Leeds United (1996-98)
782. The League Cup
783. 1944
784. 11th (during the 1998/99 season)
785. Sergei Rebrov
786. Tim Sherwood
787. 39%
788. 10th
789. Scotland
790. 2001

1996/1997
791. 7
792. Espen Baardsen
793. Southampton
794. False: Tottenham drew 1 and lost 2
795. Steffen Iversen
796. Gerry Francis
797. 13
798. John Scales
799. Sol Campbell
800. Newcastle United

ROMAN PAVLYUCHENKO
801. Russian
802. 5
803. Aston Villa
804. Bolton Wanderers
805. 9
806. Striker
807. Newcastle United
808. Blackburn Rovers
809. 1981
810. Spartak Moscow

FA CUP WINNERS - 1982
811. Ray Clemence
812. 1-0
813. Queens Park Rangers
814. Chris Hughton (Irish), Steve Archibald (Scottish) and Tony Galvin (Irish)
815. Leicester City
816. 7th

817. True: they won the FA Cup in 1981, beating Manchester City
818. Steve Perryman
819. Glenn Hoddle
820. Keith Burkinshaw

STEVE PERRYMAN
821. 1951
822. Sunderland
823. 2
824. 20
825. 2 (1981 and 1982)
826. 655: 653 (2)
827. Oxford United
828. Iceland
829. 1982
830. 31

1995/1996
831. Ruel Fox, Teddy Sheringham and David Howells
832. Chris Armstrong
833. Tottenham (8th place; Chelsea finished in 11th place)
834. 0-0
835. 16
836. Chris Armstrong
837. Gerry Francis
838. Darren Caskey
839. Leeds United
840. Darren Anderton

GUS POYET
841. Chelsea
842. Midfielder
843. Uruguay
844. 82: 66 (16)
845. Glenn Hoddle
846. Tranmere Rovers
847. Real Zaragoza
848. Portsmouth
849. Brighton & Hove Albion
850. 18

MARTIN JOL
851. 2004 (November)
852. Jacques Santini (during June 2004)
853. True (during December 2004)
854. 1956
855. 5th
856. Midfielder

857. West Bromwich Albion (1982-84) and Coventry City (1984-85)
858. Ajax
859. Juande Ramos
860. True: he won 3 full international caps for The Netherlands

1994/1995
861. Sheffield Wednesday
862. Ossie Ardiles
863. Gica Popescu
864. Nick Barmby and Teddy Sheringham
865. 4-0 to Tottenham
866. Jürgen Klinsmann
867. Tottenham (7th place; Chelsea finished 11th and Arsenal finished 12th)
868. Gudni Bergsson
869. Teddy Sheringham
870. Aston Villa

GRAHAM ROBERTS
871. 209: 200 (9)
872. True: he won 6 caps for England
873. FA Cup (1981 and 1982) and UEFA Cup (1984)
874. Chelsea
875. Central defender
876. Paul
877. Hard As Nails
878. Rangers
879. 23
880. Stoke City

1993/1994
881. Teddy Sheringham
882. Darren Caskey, Micky Hazard and Vinny Samways
883. 11
884. Ronny Rosenthal
885. Oldham Athletic
886. True
887. David Kerslake
888. Southampton
889. Jason Dozzell and Teddy Sheringham
890. Gordon Durie

PAUL ROBINSON
891. 137
892. 2004
893. Leeds United
894. Watford
895. League Cup winner (2008)

896.	41
897.	True
898.	1
899.	William
900.	Blackburn Rovers

VINNY SAMWAYS
901.	193: 165 (28)
902.	Everton
903.	True
904.	Midfielder (central)
905.	3
906.	False: he never won a full international cap, but he did play for England at under-21 level
907.	Nottingham Forest
908.	1968
909.	Walsall
910.	11

DAVID PLEAT
911.	1986/87
912.	John
913.	3rd
914.	True
915.	Luton Town
916.	1998
917.	False
918.	Winger
919.	Sheffield Wednesday
920.	1945

SQUAD NUMBERS – 2010/2011
921.	Kyle Walker	28
922.	Younes Kaboul	4
923.	Wilson Palacios	12
924.	Roman Pavlyuchenko	9
925.	Heurelho Gomes	1
926.	Sébastien Bassong	19
927.	Danny Rose	25
928.	David Bentley	5
929.	Jonathan Woodgate	39
930.	Jermaine Jenas	8

WHITE HART LANE
931.	N17 0AP
932.	Notts County
933.	1995
934.	True

935. Seven Sisters
936. Sunderland
937. 1899
938. West Stand
939. 100 metres x 67 metres
940. White Hart Lane

CLUB HISTORY
941. 1882
942. Rafael van der Vaart
943. Young Boys
944. FC Twente, Inter Milan and Werder Bremen
945. 1901
946. Peter Crouch (against Young Boys)
947. 4th
948. Bristol Rovers
949. William Gallas
950. Holsten

LEAGUE APPEARANCES - 3
951. Timothée Atouba   15 (3)
952. Young-Pyo Lee   68 (2)
953. Micky Hazard   88 (31)
954. Mark Bowen   14 (3)
955. Paul Gascoigne   91 (1)
956. Rory Allen   10 (11)
957. Chris Fairclough   60
958. Hossam Ghaly   17 (4)
959. Espen Baardsen   22 (1)
960. Andy Gray   23 (10)

SQUAD NUMBERS – 1994/1995
961. Gheorghe Popescu   4
962. Ian Walker   13
963. Sol Campbell   23
964. Ronny Rosenthal   11
965. Justin Edinburgh   3
966. Ilie Dumitrescu   8
967. David Howells   15
968. David Kerslake   22
969. Nick Barmby   7
970. Stuart Nethercott   14

LEAGUE APPEARANCES - 4
971. Gerry Armstrong   65 (19)
972. Dean Austin   117 (7)
973. Matthew Etherington   20 (25)
974. Ian Crook   10 (10)

975.	Ray Clemence	240
976.	Michael Carrick	61 (3)
977.	Colin Calderwood	152 (11)
978.	Stéphane Dalmat	12 (10)
979.	Edgar Davids	28 (3)
980.	Sean Davis	11 (4)

POSITIONS IN THE LEAGUE

981.	1980/81	10th in Division One
982.	1981/82	4th in Division One
983.	1982/83	4th in Division One
984.	1983/84	8th in Division One
985.	1984/85	3rd in Division One
986.	1985/86	10th in Division One
987.	1986/87	3rd in Division One
988.	1987/88	13th in Division One
989.	1988/89	6th in Division One
990.	1989/90	3rd in Division One

INTERNATIONALS

991.	Steve Archibald	27 Caps for Scotland
992.	Jamie Redknapp	17 Caps for England
993.	Kasey Keller	102 Caps for USA
994.	Anthony Gardner	1 Cap for England
995.	Ronny Rosenthal	60 Caps for Israel
996.	Gordon Durie	43 Caps for Scotland
997.	John Chiedozie	9 Caps for Nigeria
998.	Chris Hughton	53 Caps for Republic of Ireland
999.	Paul Walsh	5 Caps for England
1000.	Colin Calderwood	36 Caps for Scotland

2012/2013 - THE LEAGUE SEASON

1001. Reading
1002. 6 minutes
1003. Gareth Bale and Clint Dempsey
1004. Fulham
1005. Steven Caulker
1006. 5
1007. True: the nearest was Kyle Walker who played in 36 of the 38 League matches
1008. West Bromwich Albion
1009. Michael Dawson
1010. Aurasma
1011. Queens Park Rangers
1012. Jermain Defoe
1013. 5th
1014. Swansea City
1015. Jan Vertonghen

1016. True: against Aston Villa (home), Liverpool (home), Sunderland (away) and Arsenal (home)
1017. Stoke City
1018. Manchester United
1019. Emmanuel Adebayor
1020. Sunderland (the last day of the season during May 2013)
1021. Aaron Lennon
1022. True: Tottenham won 2-1 away at Sunderland
1023. Mousa Dembele
1024. 11
1025. False
1026. Southampton
1027. Emmanuel Adebayor and Gylfi Sigurdsson
1028. False
1029. 3rd
1030. Liverpool (Reading was first, finishing the season with 45 yellow cards and 1 red card)
1031. Jan Vertonghen
1032. True: the biggest win of the League season was a 4-0 away win at Aston Villa
1033. Queens Park Rangers
1034. 5th
1035. 3
1036. Manchester United (champions), Manchester City, Chelsea and Arsenal
1037. Emmanuel Adebayor
1038. Martin Jol
1039. True: 5 wins and 3 draws
1040. 72

2012/2013 - THE BOSS - ANDRE VILLAS-BOAS
1041. Harry Redknapp
1042. True: A 2-1 defeat in the Premier League, away to Newcastle United
1043. December 2012 and February 2013
1044. Chelsea
1045. 34
1046. Daniel Levy
1047. 21
1048. July
1049. Manchester United, winning at Old Trafford
1050. Portuguese

2012/2013 - STAR PLAYER - GARETH BALE
1051. 21
1052. West Ham United
1053. Sunderland
1054. 1989

1055. Aston Villa
1056. February 2013
1057. Frank
1058. 3
1059. Southampton
1060. 6 foot

2012/2013 - SQUAD NUMBERS

1061.	Gareth Bale	11
1062.	Jermain Defoe	18
1063.	Andros Townsend	31
1064.	Clint Dempsey	2
1065.	Jan Vertonghen	5
1066.	Hugo Lloris	25
1067.	Aaron Lennon	7
1068.	Brad Friedel	24
1069.	Gylfi Sigurdsson	22
1070.	Tom Huddlestone	6

2012/2013 - TRANSFERS

1071.	Lewis Holtby	Signed for Spurs from Schalke 04
1072.	Luka Modric	Signed for Real Madrid from Spurs
1073.	Jan Vertonghen	Signed for Spurs from Ajax
1074.	Rafael van der Vaart	Signed for Hamburg from Spurs
1075.	Hugo Lloris	Signed for Spurs from Lyon
1076.	Giovani Dos Santos	Signed for Mallorca from Spurs
1077.	Clint Dempsey	Signed for Spurs from Fulham
1078.	Jermaine Jenas	Signed for Queens Park Rangers from Spurs
1079.	Mousa Dembele	Signed for Spurs from Fulham
1080.	Steven Pienaar	Signed for Everton from Spurs

2012/2013 - TRIVIA – POT LUCK

1081. Coventry City
1082. Clint Dempsey
1083. False
1084. He sat to AVB's right
1085. Leeds United
1086. Investec
1087. 28
1088. Carlisle United
1089. £3.50
1090. Gareth Bale

2012/2013 - THE EUROPA LEAGUE

1091. Group J
1092. 0-0
1093. Clint Dempsey

1094. True
1095. Inter Milan
1096. True: Spurs won 2 and drew 4
1097. 2-2
1098. Clint Dempsey
1099. Jan Vertonghen
1100. Tom Huddlestone and Emmanuel Adebayor

2013/2014 - THE LEAGUE SEASON
1101. 6th
1102. December
1103. 69
1104. Emmanuel Adebayor (with 11 League goals)
1105. 2nd
1106. Emmanuel Adebayor
1107. True (away during September 2013 and at home during March 2014)
1108. Roberto Soldado
1109. Tottenham 3, Southampton 2
1110. West Bromwich Albion
1111. Fulham
1112. 3
1113. True
1114. 35,711
1115. West Ham United
1116. 37
1117. Paulinho (Spurs won 1-0)
1118. Alex Pritchard
1119. Younes Kaboul
1120. 7
1121. Milos Veljkovic
1122. True
1123. Crystal Palace
1124. Christian Eriksen
1125. Fulham
1126. West Ham United
1127. 6
1128. Andros Townsend
1129. Aston Villa
1130. Kyle Walker and Sandro
1131. Christian Eriksen
1132. Sunderland
1133. Manchester City 6 Spurs 0
1134. Mark Clattenburg
1135. West Bromwich Albion
1136. Danny Rose
1137. Everton

1138. True (as the 1992/1993 season was the first Premier League season and Spurs have remained in the top flight)
1139. Crystal Palace
1140. Hewlett-Packard (hp)

2013/2014 - THE BOSS – TIM SHERWOOD
1141. 2003
1142. Harry Redknapp
1143. True (5 wins and 1 draw)
1144. 1969
1145. Southampton
1146. 3 (all in 1999)
1147. True
1148. Bacary Sagna
1149. Portsmouth (in 2003)
1150. True

2013/2014 STAR PLAYER - EMMANUEL ADEBAYOR
1151. 10
1152. Third
1153. 21
1154. West Ham United
1155. False
1156. 38th
1157. True
1158. 6 foot 3 inches
1159. Harry Kane
1160. False (no players were sent off in the game)

2013/2014 - SQUAD NUMBERS
1161. Harry Kane   37
1162. Andros Townsend   17
1163. Danny Rose   3
1164. Jan Vertonghen   5
1165. Aaron Lennon   7
1166. Christian Eriksen   23
1167. Kyle Naughton   16
1168. Hugo Lloris   25
1169. Nabil Bentaleb   42
1170. Kyle Walker   2

2013/2014 - TRANSFERS
1171. Ajax
1172. Toronto
1173. Tom Huddlestone
1174. £26 million
1175. Erik Lamela
1176. Real Madrid

1177. Fulham
1178. FC Twente
1179. £17 million
1180. Lewis Holtby

2013/2014 - TRIVIA – POT LUCK
1181. £3.50
1182. True: Josh Onomah
1183. Arsenal
1184. True: 4 matches played (2 League matches and 2 Europa League matches)
1185. Sandro
1186. French
1187. Centre back
1188. AIA
1189. Steffen Freund
1190. False (they were knocked out in the fifth round, losing 2-1 at home to West Ham United)

2013/2014 - THE EUROPA LEAGUE
1191. Benfica
1192. Dnipro
1193. Roberto Soldado
1194. 8.05pm
1195. True (Spurs won one, drew one and lost two Europa League matches under the management of Tim Sherwood)
1196. FC Sheriff
1197. 34,283
1198. Emmanuel Adebayor
1199. False
1200. Nacer Chadli

2014/2015 - THE BOSS - MAURICIO POCHETTINO
1201. May (27th)
1202. Southampton
1203. 1972
1204. Centre back
1205. Espanyol
1206. 6 foot
1207. Argentinean
1208. West Ham United
1209. True (Two in the Premier League and two in the Europa League)
1210. 20

2014/2015 – SQUAD NUMBERS
1211. Benjamin Stambouli   25
1212. Harry Kane   18
1213. Hugo Lloris   1

1214. Erik Lamela   11
1215. Ryan Mason   38
1216. Federico Fazio   21
1217. Michael Vorm   13
1218. Paulinho   8
1219. Eric Dier   15
1220. Vlad Chiriches   6

2014/2015 - NEW SIGNINGS
1221. Eric Dier
1222. Swansea City
1223. 27 August 2014
1224. Benjamin Stambouli
1225. Sporting Lisbon
1226. Michel Vorm
1227. Goalkeeper
1228. Sevilla
1229. 1993
1230. True (away against West Ham and at home against Queens Park Rangers)

2014/2015 - POT LUCK
1231. Jesús Pérez
1232. AEL Limassol
1233. FC Schalke
1234. False
1235. Liverpool (beating Spurs 3-0 on 31 August 2014)
1236. True
1237. Hugo Lloris
1238. Sunderland
1239. £3.50
1240. Queens Park Rangers

2014/2015 - NATIONALITIES
1241. Michel Vorm   Dutch
1242. Ben Davies   Welsh
1243. Erik Lamela   Argentinean
1244. Eric Dier   English
1245. Kyle Walker   English
1246. Federico Fazio   Argentinean
1247. Brad Friedel   American
1248. Hugo Lloris   French
1249. Benjamin Stambouli   French
1250. Harry Kane   English

OTHER SPURS BOOKS
BY THE AUTHOR

The Spurs Quiz Book
Published in 2010 in hardback and 2011 as an ebook
ISBN: 9781906358860 and 9781907792434 and 9781908382740
£9.99 / £7.49

101 Interesting Facts About Spurs
Published in 2012 as an eBook
ISBN: 9781908752468 and 9781908752475
£2.49

The Gareth Bale Quiz Book
Published in 2013 as an eBook
ISBN: 9781909949898 and 9781909949904
£2.49

The Gazza Quiz Book
Published in 2013 as an eBook
ISBN: 9781909949591 and 9781909949607
£2.49

The 2012/2013 Spurs Quiz Book
Published in 2014 as an eBook
ISBN: 9781908382634 and 9781908548146
£2.49

The 2013/2014 Spurs Quiz Book
Published in 2014 as an eBook
ISBN: 9781910295854 and 9781910295861
£2.49

Lightning Source UK Ltd.
Milton Keynes UK
UKHW040616271119
354332UK00001B/200/P